BI 3107799 4

D0299276

The La...
Comprehending
Self-Mutilation

)1

...2002

24hr Renewals
0121 331 5278
or online at
http://library.uce.ac.uk

The Language of Injury: Comprehending Self-Mutilation

Gloria Babiker
and
Lois Arnold

UNIVERSITY OF
INFORMATION
SERVICES
CENTRAL ENGLAND

BPS
BOOKS The British Psychological Society

First published in 1997 by BPS Books (The British Psychological Society), St Andrews House, 48 Princess Road East, Leicester LE1 7DR, UK.

© 1997, Gloria Babiker and Lois Arnold
Reprinted 1998

All rights reserved. No part of this publication may be reproduced or transmitted, in any form or by any means, without permission.

This book is sold subject to the condition that it shall not, by way of trade or otherwise, be lent, resold, hired out, or otherwise circulated without the publisher's prior consent in any form of binding, cover, or electronic form, other than that in which it is published and without a similar condition including this condition imposed on the subsequent purchaser.

The rights of Gloria Babiker and Lois Arnold to be identified as the authors of this work have been asserted in accordance with the Copyright Designs and Patents Act, 1988.

A catalogue record for this book is available from the British Library.

ISBN 1 85433 234 1

Typeset by Poole Typesetting (Wessex) Limited
Printed in Great Britain by Arrowhead Books Limited, Reading

Whilst every effort has been made to ensure the accuracy of the contents of this publication, the publishers and authors expressly disclaim responsibility in law for negligence or any other cause of action whatsoever.

UNIVERSITY OF
CENTRAL ENGLAND

book no. 3107 7994

subject no. 616.8582/Bab

INFORMATION SERVICES

Contents

Acknowledgements

For both of us, the writing of this book came as a result of many years of learning about self-mutilation from patients, clients, and others with personal experience of injuring themselves. They have been our most important teachers and we owe them an enormous debt.

We have learned from others who work in this field and whose experience has touched ours in a variety of ways. We are grateful to many current and former colleagues at Exeter University, United Bristol Healthcare Trust, The Basement Project, and Bristol Crisis Service for Women for their numerous and varied contributions. In particular we wish to thank Professor Martin Herbert for his support with this project. We would also like to thank our editors at BPS Books, Joyce Collins and Susan Pacitti, for their help in shaping the book.

We have had the privilege of learning from mentors and supervisors, and from students, trainees and supervisees. We would like to recognize all these people for what they have taught us and helped us to understand.

Our partners, Sam Babiker and Anne Magill, who are among our most valued colleagues, have been for each of us inspiring discussants of the ideas at the basis of this book, as well as providing us with the love, support and encouragement that are indispensable in an undertaking such as this.

Finally, we wish to acknowledge and to appreciate how much we have learned from each other in the course of our collaboration.

Gloria Babiker
Lois Arnold

The conflict between the will to deny horrible events and the will to proclaim them aloud is the central dialectic of psychological trauma. People who have survived atrocities often tell their stories in a highly emotional, contradictory, and fragmented manner which undermines their credibility and thereby serves the twin imperatives of truth-telling and secrecy. When the truth is finally recognized, survivors can begin their recovery. But far too often secrecy prevails, and the story of the traumatic event surfaces not as a verbal narrative but as a symptom.

Judith L. Herman, *Trauma and Recovery*, 1992

Introduction

Our aims in writing this book are to enable practitioners, through awareness, to feel less helpless, overwhelmed, distressed and infuriated by self-injury, and more able to work confidently and effectively.

It has become apparent that there is a need for clear information about this behaviour, and for awareness to be raised that self-injury is a reflection of complex psychosocial difficulties in distressed individuals. This book is intended to be a sourcebook on self-injury or self-mutilation for practitioners and workers in the health and social services, forensic services, and the voluntary sector.

We hope that readers of this book who self-injure will find that it is helpful to their understanding and relevant to their own experiences. At the same time we acknowledge that parts of the book will be difficult to read; the very act of writing about something objectifies it, and to have one's distress objectified is painful. We hope that our empathy with the distress of those about whom we speak will come across in this book.

Workers in the field of learning disability will find the overall approach of interest because it offers a somewhat different perspective from traditional models. Through some of our work as supervisors and trainers, we have found our approach appropriate in understanding self-injury among learning disabled people, although we are not able to offer direct experience of therapeutic interventions in this particular area.

The approach that we bring to this subject is rooted in our understanding of the social basis for people's distress and the means they adopt for coping with this, as well as of the psychology of the individual. In the course of preparing this book we have become particularly interested in the fundamental significance of things to do with the body in *every* society, and the overwhelming importance of the body in a complete understanding of the 'self'.

This book represents a blending of our different backgrounds and orientations. Between us we combine formal clinical training and health service work in clinical settings (GB) with sociologically-based approaches and work in the voluntary sector (LA). In all our work we have found that the theoretical differences between us have helped each of us to clarify our thinking.

Overview of the book

Chapter 1 will introduce the topic of self-mutilation and present the parameters of our subject by defining it, reviewing current epidemiological information, and locating it within the range of other self-destructive behaviours such as parasuicide. This chapter will provide a critical review of some important thinking in the area, identifying some major themes and theoretical perspectives. We also introduce our own approach, locating this within the range of theoretical perspectives.

Chapters 2 through 4 explore the social and individual bases for self-injury, and offer a theoretical context for the rest of the book. These are not intended to be read *en bloc* necessarily, as each deals with a different aspect of the meanings and roots of this behaviour. However, individual experience and social meanings, in this and other cultures, are intertwined, and together these three chapters constitute a complete basis for understanding self-mutilation. There is reference to biological theories in *Chapter 4*, which also sets out to provide a detailed exposition of our understanding of the origins and functional nature of self-injury. This chapter constitutes the core of our understanding, and forms the basis for our recommendations towards providing services.

The final three chapters of this book deal with the issue of working with self-injury in practice. There is no definitive empirical knowledge on what works and what doesn't work in the treatment of long-term self-mutilation. We have drawn mainly on our own clinical experience and that of other specialized clinicians and authors, and have attempted to place this information into a theoretical framework, with practical guidelines for work in various settings and psychotherapy with philosophical and political elements. This we offer both to experienced workers who encounter self-mutilation regularly in their work, and to others who are struggling with the beginnings of dealing with this problem. The value of training, support and supervision in this area cannot be overstressed. Our hope is that our ideas will be considered, adapted and adjusted, and put to whatever use applies in different instances to further understanding.

Language is important and we have tried to be clear *and* respectful at the same time. In particular we have had to resolve the issue of which terms to use: *self-harm*, *self-injury*, or *self-mutilation*. We do not use the term *self-harm* because this is too broad for our purposes, as we explain in *Chapter 1*. The term *self-injury* has the advantage of being preferred to the term *self-mutilation* by individuals who struggle with this problem, and it can also encompass forms of hurting oneself which do not mutilate the body. The term *self-mutilation* is useful for the purposes of communication with other writers and practitioners in the area. Also, as will be seen from Chapters 3 and 4 particularly, the 'spoiling', or actual mutilation, of the body is a crucial part of the behaviour, and this is not reflected in the term *self-injury*. We have decided, therefore to use both terms interchangeably and hope that this will not lead to any misunderstanding or offence.

Similarly, we hope that our use of both the word 'patient' and the word 'client' will be acceptable to readers, although we do understand that both of these words have their problems. We would prefer to speak in terms of 'the person who self-injures': however, we have compromised in the interest of readability.

We will address the behaviours (cutting, burning, blows, swallowing, inserting, poisoning, picking and scratching, hair-pulling) that people carry out when they feel distressed as a means of expressing or coping with that distress. Both the behaviour and the underlying distress may or may not involve awareness on the part of the individual.

All of the examples in this book, including quotations, are drawn from actual clinical and research contacts. They have been very well modified in important details to preserve confidentiality, and cannot be traced back to any one original source. The quotes in *Chapter 4* are sometimes verbatim, with any identifying information removed. In the interest of economy, we have used the feminine pronoun throughout, but we would like to emphasize that our intention is for our approach to be relevant to both men and women. However, the reality of working in this area is that there are more women patients, and more women practitioners.

1. The Parameters of Self-Injury and Setting the Scene

More than perhaps any other human action, self-mutilation speaks of distress, torment and pain. The act of wounding oneself *embodies* – literally – an implicit connotation of something unbearable, unutterable, that is communicated in this act.

The body is essential to a sense of self. It has been referred to as the 'location of personhood' by Young (1992), who describes thus how trauma disrupts the relationship of the body to personal and social identity:

' . . . the experience of trauma also calls into question our relation to 'having a body' and 'living in a body' and makes profoundly troubling the centrality of the body in human existence . . . to live in a body and to see it as essential to one's identity, is, for the trauma survivor, both dangerous and crazy.' (p.92)

Self-injury expresses how 'dangerous and crazy' it is to be in a physical body which is traumatized. In this book we will make many links between abuse trauma and self-injury. One of the most distressing and desperate features of abuse is its demand for secrecy and silence; victims who wish and long to be heard are forbidden from speaking by various means. For such people, self-injury expresses, if only for oneself, the horrors of abuse.

The conflict between speaking and not speaking is described by Judith Herman (1992) as the conflict between the will to deny horrible events and the will to proclaim them out loud. People who have awful things to recount sometimes reflect this conflict by doing so in such a way as to undermine their own credibility. In these terms, self-inflicted injuries, while telling an 'unspeakable secret', can also be used to deflect attention from it. Thus self-mutilation is used at once to speak and not speak.

Suicide and attempted suicide are forms of communication also, to the extent that they may be a message to others, but self-mutilation

1

demands to be listened to in a different way. Self-mutilation provides primarily an expression to *oneself* and then to others, of traumatic experience and distress. Self-injury *continues* the discourse of a person's life, whereas a suicide attempt *separates* the person from that discourse, removing the individual from their awareness or from being. Perhaps the difference lies in the fact that a suicide attempt primarily seeks to alter consciousness, but self-mutilation alters the body. Talk ceases during altered consciousness, but not in behaviours that involve the language of the body. Walsh and Rosen (1988) in discussing the difference between self-mutilation and parasuicide have noted:

'In the case of ingesting pills or poison, the harm caused is uncertain, ambiguous, unpredictable, and basically invisible. In the case of self-lacerations, the degree of self-harm is clear, unambiguous, predictable as to course, and highly visible.' (p.32)

Self-injury is one part of a large repertoire of behaviours *that involve the body* in the expression of distress within the individual. Self-mutilation, as one of these behaviours, also offers a means for the individual to attempt to deal with the distress. As we shall see in the next two chapters, self-mutilation is also one of many practices whose historical, political and cultural significance involve modification or damage to the body, thus fulfilling many functions for the individual *and* for society.

In this chapter we aim to set the scene for our discussion of self-injury and ways of responding to it. We begin by delineating our area of concern, that is, the behaviours which for us fall within the terms 'self-injury' and 'self-mutilation', and setting these within the context of a broad spectrum of behaviours which involve some degree of harm to the body. We go on to briefly review some of the major strands in thinking about self-injury. In this we aim primarily to establish where we ourselves stand with respect to the range of theoretical perspectives on this behaviour, and to introduce some of the ideas on which we have drawn in developing our own approach to self-injury. In one chapter we cannot do justice to all these perspectives, and some (approaches concerning psychiatric diagnoses in particular) we visit only briefly, hoping readers will follow up their own interests through the references.

Self-Injury: A Definitional Approach

We understand self-injury as an act which involves deliberately inflicting pain and/or injury to one's own body, but without suicidal intent. The most common form of self-injury is cutting, often of the arms and hands, perhaps of the legs, and less commonly of the face, torso, breasts, and genitals. Some people burn or scald themselves, others inflict blows on their bodies, or bang themselves against something. Some people inflict different sorts of injury upon themselves at different times, depending upon their feelings and what is available to them.

Other ways in which people injure themselves include: scratching, picking, biting, scraping, and occasionally inserting sharp objects under the skin or into body orifices. Less common forms of self-injury include tying ligatures, pulling out one's hair and eyelashes and scrubbing oneself so hard as to cause abrasion (sometimes using cleansers such as bleach). Some people swallow sharp objects or harmful substances.

Our definitional approach compares self-injury to other forms of apparently self-destructive behaviour (see *Figure 1*), such as self-harm (parasuicide), eating disorders, substance abuse and factitious disorders. Self-injury belongs in this wider category of behaviours, because they are all tied together by some degree of harmfulness to the body. On the other hand, self-injury may be distinguished from other destructive behaviours in various important ways, such as lethality, social construction, intention, purpose, directness and immediacy of injury, whether illness is a focus, and whether there is any deception involved. As discussed in the preface, we use the terms self-mutilation and self-injury interchangeably, but we are aware that they have different connotations for different people, and that one or the other is preferred by different approaches.

Self-mutilation versus body 'enhancement'

We consider that there are two types of body enhancement. The first type consists of behaviours which are socially prescribed and designed to enable the individual to attain some 'ideal' of physical 'attractiveness'. This applies mainly to women, but increasingly to men. Examples include breast enlargement and other cosmetic surgery, some degree of body piercing, hair removal and the wearing of corsets. There are also racial aspects to this type of behaviour when the purpose is to attain a western ideal of beauty. Examples here would include skin bleaching and hair straightening among African women, and facial surgery among Oriental women. Body enhancement differs from self-injury in its total social acceptance. It is seen as serving as a testimony to someone's level of functioning and consideration of themselves as 'worth' the effort and expense. On the other hand, we think it important to point out that this type of body 'enhancing' behaviour is very similar to self-injury in one

	Self-destructive behaviours *e.g.* *eating disorders* *substance abuse* *sexual risk-taking*	
Somatic expressions of feeling *e.g.* *skin disorders* *pain* *accident-proneness*		**Body 'enhancement'** *e.g.* *cosmetic surgery* *tatooing* *piercing* *bleaching*
	Self-injury/ mutilation *e.g.* *cutting, scraping* *burning* *banging, hitting*	
Factitious disorders *e.g.* *Munchausen's syndrome* *simulated illness* *polysurgery*		**Self-harm** *e.g.* *suicide* *parasuicide* *overdosing*
	Other/marginal self-injurious behaviours *e.g.* *smoking* *reckless driving* *workaholism* *danger sports*	

Figure 1. Self-injury in the context of other behaviours involving harm to the body.

important respect: it always contains as an underlying assumption the individual's belief that they are somehow not good enough without modification of their body.

The second type consists of behaviours whose social relevance lies not in their aesthetic appeal, but in their ability to challenge social convention and in some cases to shock or to define marginal social groups. Examples here would include head shaving, extensive tattooing, and piercing unusual parts of the body. Compared with self-injury, our view is that this is much more about a message than about the injurious act itself. That is to say that the end result, and the message that it carries, are often more important than what the individual has to undergo in the way of injury to their body. However, part of the message may be to do with the pain and endurance and courage, and either pride or self-hatred involved in the act. It may also be that the act of *submitting* to this injury and the pain involved may carry deep relationship meanings and function in similar ways to self-mutilation. Similarities between this type of behaviour and self-injury can be in communication of anger and an 'in your face' imposing of an identity or a position. In certain populations these similarities are very powerful. Harry (1987) compared male offenders with and without tattoos and found that those with tattoos tended also to bear scars of self-mutilation.

It seems to us that both types of body 'enhancement', or acceptable mutilation, like self-injury, contain elements of self-hatred. Both types can also include elements of belonging or aspiring to belong to a group that the individual values.

Self-mutilation versus self-destructive behaviours

Self-mutilation is similar to other apparently *self-destructive* behaviours such as eating disorders, alcohol abuse, sexual risk-taking, or repeated elective surgery but also has important differences from these. Writers who focus narrowly on the link between these behaviours and childhood sexual trauma, tend to include all such behaviours in the same category (Miller, 1994).

Ross and McKay (1979) make the distinction between direct and indirect self-injurious behaviour. In the case of direct self-injury, the link between the behaviour and the consequence (that is, a wound) is immediate and unequivocal, while in the case of indirect self-injurious behaviours (such as eating disorders and substance abuse) this link is remote and equivocal.

Amongst eating behaviours, extreme obesity in our opinion shares the most elements with self-mutilation, including that of rebellion against traditional ideals of feminine emotional responding, and vomiting seems the most immediately self-injurious behaviour. Whilst many authors (for example, Favazza *et al.*, 1989) focus on the similarities between self-mutilation and eating difficulties, in our view it is important to recognize their differences in terms of their functions for the individual and for society.

The self-destructive element contained in behaviours such as sexual risk-taking leads one to notice obvious parallels with self-mutilation, notably its function as a distraction from immediate distress or its use in self-punishment. Self-injury shares its function as a distracter from distress with alcohol and drug abuse, but is far less socially problematic, whilst at the same time being 'madder' and outside the normal range of how people cope with distress. Alcohol and drug abuse simply constitute normal social behaviour 'gone too far', except in the case of intravenous drug use, which is interesting in this respect. The physical 'needle in the flesh' is an important aspect of the habit for many users, and of course constitutes direct injury to the body. Although vilified and marginalized, drug injecting is nevertheless not usually seen as 'mad' in the way self-mutilation is. Unlike self-injury, this category

5

of self-destructive behaviours has the primary purpose of absenting oneself from pain rather than of doing something to oneself.

It is frequently the case that self-injury occurs in individuals who also have problems with substance abuse and/or eating (Favazza *et al.*, 1989; Lacey, 1993; Parkin and Eagles,1993). Some authors (for example, Favazza et al. (1989), have argued for the use of special labels (usually 'impulse'-based definitions) to describe these combinations. To some extent, there can be a trade-off between self-destructive behaviours in these combinations, with one becoming less of a problem as another worsens. In our view, it does not add to the understanding of self-injury and its meaning, to see it any differently when it is part of a 'syndrome'. Favazza and Rosenthal (1993) have reported that their 'multi-impulsive' patients claim that alcohol abuse is the easiest of these behaviours to overcome, and self-mutilation the hardest. We also find this to be the case in our clinical experience. There are possibly two aspects to this: one is that self-mutilation is very difficult to live without, but also it can seem to be the most benign choice out of the many means individuals could use to cope and survive. One patient described how, for her, eating was only possible because she knew she could injure herself afterwards: 'I have to eat to stay alive, and I have to cut myself so that I can manage to eat.'

Self-injury versus self-harm

Self-injury is often seen as a part of the *'self-harm'* or *'deliberate self-harm'* category which also includes parasuicide and suicide. Walsh and Rosen (1988) have presented what may be the most comprehensive and erudite review of thinking on the differences between self-mutilation and suicide/parasuicide. It is now generally accepted by authors who work clinically in this area (for example Briere, 1996; Favazza and Rosenthal, 1993; Tantam and Whittaker, 1992) that there is an important difference between attempted suicide and self-injury, and that this difference is fairly clear: in attempted suicide the person intends to kill himself, in self-injury the person does not. However, our view is that an excessively simplistic adherence to this distinction is problematic, as it ignores the fact that often what is presented as a suicide attempt, for instance an overdose, does not in fact involve an intention to die. The individual may have complex and ambivalent, and also confused, views of their exact intent. Individuals who frequently self-injure may also at some other times harm themselves with suicidal intent, often using different means.

Correspondingly, someone who self-injures, whilst having no suicidal intent, may have such self-hatred and despair as to wish to destroy and annihilate any real experience of self, in order to carry on functioning at some other level. The danger is to view self-injury as somehow less serious than suicide attempts, and not to respond to the despair and the profoundly troubled self that it contains.

Kreitman (1977) has pointed out that while a clear definition of the difference between attempted suicide and other forms of self-injury (which he refers to as self-mutilation) can be attempted in conceptual terms, the empirical definition is fraught with difficulties. We would contend that while it may seem easy to distinguish between self-injury and suicide on the basis of lethality, intent, and so on, it is altogether more complex to distinguish between self-injury and repeated, minor self-harming or parasuicide behaviour.

Although the difference between suicide and self-mutilation is often elaborated by researchers and practitioners, and the distinction between the two considered important (Walsh and Rosen, 1988), many practitioners and clinical writers see them as similar, in that both suicide and self-injury are considered reflections of self-destructiveness (Linehan, 1993). In our view however, the person who self-mutilates can be said in some ways to be carrying out the very *reverse* of self-destructiveness. They are seeking to preserve themselves. Rather than wishing to destroy themselves, their self-injury helps them to stay 'together', to struggle to survive.

Self-mutilation versus factitious disorders

Illness or injury can sometimes be a means of avoiding extremely stressful or dangerous situations, such as direct combat during war; or of bringing about changes in one's circumstances, for example, a transfer to better living conditions. These are fairly straightforward examples, where individuals may bring about their own injuries or make themselves ill as an instrumental means of achieving another end. We do not see this behaviour as resulting from an awareness of psychological distress in the same way as is self-injury. However, factitious disorders are more complex as they involve entering into a medical relationship via the sick role. As with self-injury, this may often be a means of meeting relational needs, and coping through physical means. In this sense, we see that factitious disorder may involve self-injury, not as an end in itself, but more as a means to an end.

In the case of self-injury it would appear that people are more aware of their psychological agony, and make or tell of the connection between their distress and the injuring. People with factitious disorders on the other hand, do not explain, or even seem to understand, their illness behaviour in psychological terms. This behaviour is carried out primarily in adoption of the 'sick role', which defines the quality of the interaction that the individual wants with other people. Its primary aim is to produce symptoms, and it is frequently accompanied by elaborate manufactured stories about the individual's illness, life and identity ('pseudologia fantastica'). Carers working with the resulting symptoms have to track down their cause detective-fashion (see Feldman and Ford (1994) for a discussion of factitious disorders). In comparison, self-injury is often private, not carried out primarily with the aim of eliciting a response from others, and where it does come to light, there is rarely any pretence that the individual did not do it to herself. Individuals who self-injure are far more likely to be self-effacing than they are to tell lengthy stories featuring themselves as heroic victim. One similarity between self-injury and factitious disorders may be that the individuals concerned are extremely angry at caregivers. However, people with factitious disorders may express this anger by 'outsmarting' caregivers, whilst with self-injury, what operates is more akin to defiance.

Sometimes a factitious disorder involves harm to others, adult to child or adult to adult, for example, where a caregiver induces symptoms in their dependant in order to obtain medical attention. As with the other kind of factitious disorders, and sometimes with self-injury, the individuals involved are reduced to such behaviour by the conviction (and perhaps even the experience) that only this sort of behaviour will produce the attention and concern from caregivers for which they long.

Self-mutilation versus somatic expressions of feeling

Although we do not propose to cover this area in a comprehensive way, throughout this book we will emphasize the importance of an understanding of somatic expressions of feeling in the context of a human response to distress. Many people somatize rather than speak, and produce physical pain at moments when they cannot tolerate psychic pain. This can range from what most people would recognize as 'psychosomatic' or 'stress-related' illnesses (for example, headaches), where psychological factors impact on a recognized medical condition, all the way to extremely serious conditions such as blindness or paralysis for which there is no apparent physical cause. As we shall see in *Chapter 3*, distress can be expressed through women's bodies via the normal functions of menstruation and childbearing, and expressing distress through these functions has a powerful psychological impact (see, for example, Pines (1993)). In terms of a definitional comparison between self-mutilation and somatic expressions of feeling, the most obvious difference concerns the extent of conscious awareness that is involved in bringing about changes in the condition of the body. In individuals with psychosomatic disorders, the physical manifestations are not intentional, nor under voluntary control, as they usually are in self-mutilation. The attribution of distress however, is probably the most fundamental difference between the two. In individuals with somatoform complaints, the physical aspect usually appears to the individual to be the cause or signal of their distress, whereas for individuals who self-mutilate, the physical aspect *follows*, and appears to be the means to cope with psychological distress.

Self-injury versus other/marginal self-injurious behaviours

Human beings engage in a huge range of socially acceptable behaviours for various purposes which involve some degree of harm or threat to the body. Even where such behaviours are disapproved or subject to sanctions (for example, reckless driving, fighting) they are not seen as 'mad' in the same way as self-injury is. Some behaviours, such as overwork, are socially applauded or rewarded, even though their potentially damaging consequences are known.

The major difference between these behaviours and self-injury is often in intention; the behaviour may be extremely damaging to the body (for example, smoking), yet unlike self-injury the damage is not its primary purpose. Instead, the aim may be pleasure and excitement, for example in dangerous sports, or competition and achievement of social status, as in overwork or fighting. On the face of it these are very different from what someone seeks through self-injury, although all of these outcomes may in fact also be encompassed within the functions of self-injury for some individuals. Where such behaviours share more common ground with self-injury is in the less obvious functions which they may fulfil for some individuals. For example, smoking, like self-injury, may be a means of coping and comforting oneself at times of distress. Overwork or dangerous sports, like self-mutilation, may function as a means of distraction from uncomfortable feelings. Reckless driving or fighting can be a means, like self-injury for others, of expressing anger, despair and frustration. One important difference between self-injury and other marginal injurious behaviours may be in the attitude to the self which is reflected by the individual concerned. Where self-hatred, or at least lack of care for oneself, is involved, there is more similarity to self-injury. Where pride and self-fulfilment are evident (for example, where an individual engages with due care in a risky sport which enhances their life), the difference from self-injury is more marked. However, even this is not so straightforward as it seems. As we shall see in *Chapter 4*, self-injury can for some people be a means of attempting to enhance a sense of self or of asserting strength and endurance.

Incidence and Prevalence of Self-Injury

There is surprisingly little clear epidemiological information on the incidence and prevalence of self-injury in the general population. We feel that this reflects in part the secrecy and lack of understanding surrounding the behaviour. In the absence of a clear definition, furthermore, self-injury gets confounded with medical diagnoses such as Borderline Personality Disorder, and, in the normal population with suicide behaviour and overdosing. Estimates of the incidence of self-injury vary widely, with a recent review (Favazza and Rosenthal, 1993) reporting estimates of its prevalence ranging from 400 to 1400 per 100,000 population per year. It has been suggested that at least one in 600 people injure themselves sufficiently to need hospital treatment (Tantam and Whittaker, 1992). This excludes those (probably many) who present their injuries as accidental. There is considerable under-reporting, with many people hiding self-injury even from their families and never coming to the attention of health practitioners. Confidential helplines receive calls from people who have injured themselves for years without telling anyone, due to shame and fear of condemnation.

Walsh and Rosen (1988) reviewed a range of approaches to determining the incidence of self-injury, but concluded that 'Determining precisely the incidence of self-mutilation is difficult if not impossible at present'. The difficulty arises from both severe under-reporting and from great variation in the nature of such studies as have been carried out to determine incidence. Many epidemiological studies (for example, Morgan (1979)) have included very wide ranges of behaviour, including overdoses, and self-poisoning. A few studies which focused on self-mutilation were *under-inclusive*, counting only wrist-cutting (for example, Weissman, 1975).

It would seem, therefore, that what is desperately needed in this area is systematic empirical work to establish the prevalence of self-mutilation and to examine its link with childhood and adult experience. John Briere and his colleagues (1995, personal communication) are currently in the course of reporting such empirical work. In a study carried out on a non-clinical university population, Briere and his colleagues (1990) found that 11 per cent of students questioned had slashed or cut themselves at some point in their lives. This research continues with other groups.

Often people report that their self-injury began in childhood, with scratches and bumps being disguised as 'accidents', progressing to more systematic cutting, burning and so on in adolescence. It is important that professionals working with children and young people are aware of self-injury, so that the problem can be picked up quickly. This is especially so given that self-injury almost always occurs in response to serious problems, such as abuse, in a young person's life.

Self-injury is often seen as a problem affecting younger adults and it is less often reported amongst people of middle age and later years. However, we know that self-injury sometimes carries on for many years, so that older adults *must* also be harming themselves. It is not yet clear whether the apparent rarity of self-injury amongst older people is real (perhaps because people stop self-injuring as they mature), or whether the difference is due to under-reporting. It may be that the stigma and shame associated with self-injury (and the problems underlying it) affect reporting by older people even more. Again, this may lead to a failure to identify and respond to people's distress.

Selected Perspectives on Self-Injury

Psychiatric diagnosis and self-injury

Psychiatric diagnoses stem from a structuralist approach; that is, one where the main emphasis is on classification, or assigning 'problem' behaviours to a category. People who express extreme distress through the body often receive one of two problematic diagnoses: Borderline Personality Disorder if they self-injure, and Somatization Disorder (this diagnosis was once known as 'hysteria') if they produce non-self-inflicted physical symptoms. These two diagnoses are probably most frequently applied to survivors of childhood sexual abuse, although evidence for the link between somatization disorder and childhood trauma is not as strong as that for the link between abuse and borderline personality disorder (see Briere, 1996 and Herman, 1992). In addition, in a manner similar to self-injury; individuals with these diagnoses appear to provoke very strong reactions amongst practitioners. In this section we will concentrate mainly on the 'borderline' diagnosis, as it is related directly to self-injury. The approach presented in this book is generally at odds with the culture of psychiatric diagnosis as it applies to self-mutilation. However, as we shall discuss at length elsewhere, our approach can be carried out productively in psychiatric settings. In the cause of working together in the best interests of patients, it is important to look for common ground and compatibility.

Self-injury at the borderline

The borderline diagnosis is one of the controversial issues of contemporary mental health work. The very term 'borderline' is fraught with difficulties of different sorts; many who do accept the term nevertheless point out that it is not clear what it actually refers *to* (for example, Gunderson and Singer, 1986): a condition, a syndrome, a patient, or, in psychoanalytic terms, a form of personality organization (as in Kernberg, 1967).

Diagnoses such as Borderline Personality Disorder (and this includes the criteria in DSM-IV) are in fact somewhat circular, in that they consist of descriptive accounts of features associated with the behaviour of individuals who receive the diagnosis. There has been considerable disagreement (see Gunderson and Singer, 1986), within this approach on what constitutes the specific characteristics of this condition. The characteristic on which there is the most agreement, however, and that is most frequently associated with the behaviour of patients described as 'borderline', is that of *impulsiveness* or *self-destructiveness* (typically self-injury). Gunderson and Singer (1986) have clarified that it is usually the *result* rather than the purpose of the behaviour that is self-destructive. They write, 'generally , borderline patients do not regard these behaviours as self-destructive, self-degradive, or guilt provoking'. In our experience, it is true that individuals often do not see their self-injury as self-destructive, but they frequently *do* experience it as degrading or guilt-provoking.

Marsha Linehan has focused her research and clinical activity in this area, adopting what she terms a 'biosocial' approach that stresses the interaction of biological and social learning influences on 'borderline individuals who have histories of multiple attempts to injure, mutilate, or kill themselves' (Linehan, 1993). Elsewhere she refers to the 'behavioural speciality' of Borderline Personality Disorder as 'a pattern of intentional self-damaging acts and suicide attempts'. Linehan proposes that the two most important social influences that are likely to facilitate this picture are what she terms an 'invalidating environment', and sexism. An 'invalidating environment' in Linehan's terms is one where the communication of private experiences is met with unreliable, inappropriate, or extreme responses. It is important to note that what Linehan considers significant is that the *expression* of private experiences is not validated, instead being trivialized or punished. Expressions of distress might be attributed to unacceptable characteristics on the part of the individual, or the individual may be told that they are wrong to be feeling as they are.

Linehan argues that a formulation of social influences on Borderline Personality Disorder must include sexism, as the diagnosis applies primarily to women (76 per cent). The relationship between the picture of self-damage described by Linehan as Borderline Personality Disorder and what she terms sexism is sketchy, particularly as Linehan includes sexual abuse as the primary form of what she terms sexism. Interestingly, it appears to be in the *secrecy* demanded by sexual abuse that Linehan finds the link with self-harming behaviour. One might criticize Linehan for writing on these issues in a seeming absence of awareness of the important sociological feminist literature on the subject. She may also, perhaps as a result, be somewhat tentative in describing the influence of social variables on Borderline Personality Disorder, but the fact that she does it at all is commendable. Her approach to delivering therapy to this population, which we will refer to again elsewhere, is also innovative among primarily structuralist approaches in its advocacy above all of validating the patient's experience and the injunction that 'the main thing is to avoid blaming the victim'.

Self-mutilation and somatization

Judith Herman (1992) points out that, up to a century ago, there was awareness through the work of Paul Briquet of the link between Somatization Disorder (or frequent, multiple somatic complaints, sometimes also called Briquet's Syndrome) in children, and these children being maltreated and held in fear by their parents, or with other traumatic experiences. The DSM-IV diagnosis of Somatization Disorder is made on the basis of a list of symptoms which must include at least four different sites of pain, two gastrointestinal symptoms, one sexual symptom (this includes reproductive symptoms) and one pseudo-neurological or 'conversion' symptom. DSM-IV also adds to this list the information: 'They are often inconsistent historians (and) the lives of these individuals . . . are often as chaotic and complicated as their medical histories'. People (nearly always women) who receive the diagnosis 'Somatization Disorder' often accumulate many other diagnoses as well, for example anxiety, depression, and further diagnoses of personality disorders, in addition to their numerous physical complaints. It seems to us that specific information about this condition is lacking to such an extent as to make it almost incomprehensible. We are proposing that the only way of understanding this huge constellation of variables is to recognize its functional nature. Somatic disorder may be a means by which distress arising from childhood maltreatment is expressed through the body.

The clinical approach

The literature in this area encompasses work referring to 'deliberate self-harm' (Morgan, 1979), 'self-injury', 'self-mutilation', and, more rarely, other terms such as 'self-wounding' (Tantam and Whittaker, 1992). The 'self-harm' literature tends to conflate suicide, para-suicide and self-injury. A literature search on the term 'self-injury' would yield a large number of references written mainly about populations with learning disabilities. The term 'self-mutilation' is used very widely in the mental health and feminist literature to denote non-suicidal intentional self-injury. Some mental health and feminist literature (mainly in this country) uses the term 'self-injury' to reflect the language preferred by service-users.

The major work in the area of writing about self-injury takes what might be called a clinical approach; that is, one that pathologizes self-mutilation, seeing it as an aberration, a maladjustment, a disorganization of normal functioning, or illness. Self-injury has been seen variously as manifestations of personality or character disorder (for example, Walsh and Rosen, 1988; Favazza and Rosenthal, 1993); a disorder of impulse control (Favazza, 1992; Pattison and Kahan, 1983); and a multi-impulsive personality disorder (Lacey and Evans, 1986). Tantam and Whittaker (1992) argue a case for recognition of a 'deliberate self-harm syndrome', but criticize personality disorder diagnoses, arguing that there is no personality disorder unique to self-wounding and noting that, 'The attribution of upsetting behaviour to abnormal personality tends to blunt the normal caring response . . . Too often, further inquiry into the reasons for the behaviour, in particular into the situational determinants of self-wounding, stops once a diagnosis is made'.

Whilst traditionally the approach has been structuralist, elements of a functionalist understanding are being introduced. Increasingly, proponents of such an understanding recognize readily that self-mutilation constitutes a symptom of underlying distress and serves many functions for the individual in coping with that distress; however, the over-riding view is that the behaviour represents a symptom of mental ill health that must be treated. This is largely understandable in one sense: self-mutilation, which is normally private to the individual and carried out in secret, nevertheless frequently reveals itself in the context of extreme psychological distress, in individuals having received psychiatric diagnoses such as we have noted. This approach, while not particularly helpful to the individual, nor as we shall see, effective in stopping self-injury, is nevertheless relatively straightforward. In this context, there is already a pathology 'package' and self-mutilation is one among many 'symptoms' to be brought under control.

What is less straightforward about this clinical approach, is that it seems aimed at helping individuals who are suffering, but may actually be aimed at those aspects of the *expression* of their suffering that workers find especially difficult: 'You may express your agony, but not in *this* language'.

Self-injury provokes very strong reactions amongst practitioners, fellow clients and patients, family members and friends of people who harm themselves. Frances (1987) reported that 'Of all disturbing patient behaviours, self-mutilation is the most difficult for clinicians to understand and to treat. . . . The typical clinician (myself included) treating a patient who self-mutilates is often left feeling a combination of helpless, horrified, guilty, furious, betrayed, disgusted and sad'. It seems frequently to be the case that even professionals who have little difficulty in working with people who attempt suicide, starve themselves or engage in harmful addictive behaviours, find self-mutilation extremely distressing and unacceptable.

Intentional damage to the body seems an extremely difficult form of expression for health workers to process. As such, we need to recognize that in carrying out our resolute clinical assumptions about self-mutilation we are seeking to deal with our own difficulties in accepting this behaviour. Medical healthcare professionals operate a very plain language of healing and reparation of the body, and respect for the integrity of the body: injuries have to be fixed to make the body whole. The problem with self-injury is that if one, as a medical professional, does not intervene, the body and the person are not 'fixed'.

A primarily clinical approach offers drugs that are meant to address self-injury, behavioural management and psychological therapy programs to bring it under control, and psychotherapies that are designed to achieve the cessation of self-mutilation (Rockland, 1987; Linehan, 1993). Usually there is an explicit ban against the behaviour, which is monitored, even if only covertly, and frequently the continuation of treatment is contingent on the continued declared abstention from self-injury.

Psychoanalytic thinking on self-destructiveness

The psychoanalytic approach to the understanding of self-mutilation has not presented a single unified view but rather a variety of views from different aspects. Menninger's (1938) book, *Man against Himself*, was the first significantly comprehensive work in this area and has been extremely influential. Menninger classified as self-mutilation a huge spectrum of behaviours, ranging from nail-biting through 'purposive' accidents, malingering and polysurgery to the most extreme and bizarre forms of self-injury. Menninger explained self-mutilation as a 'focal suicide' which he defined as a partial suicide, or a compromise. Menninger was influenced by Franz Alexander who wrote his paper *The Need for Punishment and the Death Instinct* in 1929 (cited in Menninger, 1938) to elaborate Freud's idea of the death instinct. In this framework, self-mutilation is a compromise of sorts between the life and the death instincts leading to the 'postponement' of the death instinct in which the impulse to destroy the self is diluted. In common with nearly all of the subsequent psychoanalytic writers on this topic, Menninger theorized *similarities* between self-mutilation and suicide, and did not address the issue of the *differences* between the two. Menninger described the act of actual suicide as containing three components: murder of the self, murder by the self and the element of dying. He then writes of acts of self-mutilation:

'They are determined in general by the same motives and mechanisms outlined for suicide proper except in the participation of the death instinct.'

One of the most influential of Menninger's ideas has been the breaking down of suicide and 'focal suicide' into the three aspects of *the wish to kill, the wish to be killed* and *the wish to die.* Psychoanalytic writers since then have agreed that people who self-mutilate have problems in both areas of outwardly and inwardly directed aggression The interplay between the self-punitive and destructive components was taken up by Mollon (1996) who described the 'state of helplessness' that prompts individuals to self-mutilate. Mollon writes:

'The person who is deliberately cutting the body has entered a private world of omnipotence in which s/he is both abuser and abused . . . Overwhelming rage is this way discharged on the body, which is thereby 'punished' for being a victim of abuse.' (page 71)

The area of sexuality and self-mutilation as containing an erotic element has also been highlighted by psychoanalytic writers. Menninger conceived of self-mutilation as a form of price that has to be paid for indulgence in 'forbidden' activity such as masturbation. Subsequent interpretations of the meaning of self-mutilation have also often featured masturbation, symbolic castration (see Favazza, 1987) for a comprehensive review), or symbolic menstruation (Stone, 1987). Estella Weldon (1996) suggests that women attack their own bodies as a means of releasing unbearable (sexual) anxiety. Weldon has pointed out that men act out their 'perversions' in this way against others, while women are much more likely to act against themselves.

   Writers in this field commonly find the antecedents of self-injury in some form of loss or separation (Walsh and Rosen, 1988). Stone (1987) has delineated this as mostly traumatic loss, or a traumatic death where the horror is relived and the death itself is denied through self-injury. Janine Chasseguet-Smirgel (1990) has described such patients (whom she terms 'psychosomatic') as unable to tolerate the psychic or physical absences of a 'love partner' (that is, mother) and 'unable to bear the idea that the other's mind may be occupied by thoughts not centering on themselves'. This leads them to 'states of dereliction, rage and despair' such that they are always 'seeking a way back to the mother's body' through self-destructive acts.

16

The theme of attribution to others, or a 'theory of mind' as it applies in the area of self-injury, has been one of the most creative developments in psychoanalytic thinking. Fonagy and Target (1995) suggest that self-harm and aggression towards others reflect an impoverishment in the capacity to 'mentalize' (that is, to think and conceptualize). In some patients, in whom there is a wish to attack the self and others, Fonagy and Target suggest 'the underlying motive is the same: *a wish to attack thoughts, in oneself or in another*' (italics theirs).

Violence towards the self in Fonagy and Target's terms may reflect a failure to match one's mind with the mind of the other, to understand the mental state of the other; put at its simplest, to see things from the other's point of view. Fonagy (1991) suggested that childhood maltreatment may lead to an impairment of the capacity to see things from the point of view of another. This may develop as a defence against the realization that an abusive other could *know* the effect on me of what they are doing to me and yet do it anyway. To reach a healthy capacity to mentalize means accepting that others can hold ideas about me and see things from my point of view, in ways that are not perceived by me as persecutory and intrusive. When this capacity to mentalize is impaired, and Fonagy and Target are clear that one of the ways this can happen is through childhood maltreatment, then language and symbolic communication are no longer adequate. So the individual becomes forced to resort to communication through the body. The authors describe this as 'the use of the bodily self as a refuge . . . and bodily experiences to provide a sense of consolidation'.

While there appears on the surface to be considerable diversity among psychoanalytic writers in this area, this applies mainly to the interpretation of the *meaning* of the act of self-mutilation. The functions of the act for individuals are much less frequently addressed. And yet, in our experience, when people who self-injure describe the centrality of this activity in their lives, they invariably do so in terms of its functions. A further problem is that the interpretations offered are frequently experienced as offensive or irrelevant. This may account for the lack of sympathy, until recent theoretical shifts towards abuse-oriented formulations, between psychoanalytic approaches and individuals who self-mutilate. Nevertheless, this body of work offers us important avenues in our understanding of self-mutilation which we will take up in this book. We will return to themes which contribute towards a conceptualization of expression through the body, when symbolic means of communication (that is thinking and language) are inadequate; and to the ways that this can happen as a result of childhood maltreatment.

Systems and family thinking

Self-mutilation may serve functions for a family (or couple), as well as for the individual. The behaviour may reflect difficulties and distress in the whole family or relationship, yet confines any attribution of disturbance or fault to the individual who is self-injuring. Attention and help may be attracted by self-injury in a member of the 'system', without the need for the remainder of the 'system' to invest personally.

Mary Louise Wise (1989) and Fossum and Mason (1986) developed a model of a 'shame-bound cycle' in abusive families where compulsive control leads to abusive release in an attempt to escape the shame and control. Self-mutilation in individual family members is one of the routes of escape from shame-bound control which Fossum and Mason list.

The difference between self-mutilation and suicidality has been addressed in this area also. Senior (1988) has suggested that the families of suicidal adolescents and non-suicidal self-mutilating adolescents present distinct, identifiable dynamics, each of which requires a special treatment intervention. Families of adolescents who self-injure are seen by Senior as enmeshed, symbiotic, and internally directed, with poor boundaries that do not allow members to make outside alliances. In contrast, the therapist's observation was that of mutual distance and affective disengagement between the suicidal adolescents and their parents.

Aldridge (1988) suggests that within a psychiatric hospital setting self-mutilation is a systemic (or collective pattern of) behaviour. He observed a circular pattern whereby increasing confusion and conflict between nursing and medical hierarchies was followed by episodes of increased self-mutilation by patients, which served temporarily to clarify staff roles and reduce conflict by uniting staff. The suggestion is that within such settings it is more fruitful to address self-mutilation as a response to distress within the whole system (of patients and staff), rather than confining the formulation of the problem to the individual patients. Our own formulation of the role of self-mutilation in a culture is expanded in *Chapters 2* and *3*. In our terms, the patients on a ward may be carrying and serving a particular culture via their self-mutilation. It is important to be sensitive, however, to the difficulties for staff in seeing themselves as playing a causal part in patients' self-mutilation, and systemic approaches such as this underline the need to frame one's understanding of self-injury in a non-blaming way.

Community and political approaches

Feminist thinking and therapy have been paramount amongst socially-motivated approaches to human distress. The feminist approach is not dissimilar to the clinical approach in that it stresses the idea that self-injury is a way of coping with difficulties. Where the starting point for the clinical approach is the individual, however, the feminist approach stresses the inequalities between the experience of men and women as well as that of the members of various other social groups. Burstow (1992) argues that in a patriarchal society all women engage in some type of bodily self-injury (such as hair removal), and indeed are encouraged to do so. She goes on to make the point that the term 'self-mutilation' is generally used to refer exclusively to forms or degrees of self-injury that are not socially condoned. All other (that is, condoned) forms or degrees of self-injury are essentially not seen as injurious. We wish to emphasize the importance of Burstow's view that self-mutilation includes a 'spoiling' quality, which may reflect a defiance of oppressive rules about beauty and the female body. This understanding of self-injury will be expanded in *Chapter 3*.

User and 'survivor' perspectives on self-injury (Harrison, 1996; Pembroke, 1995) frequently emphasize the validity of self-injury as a creative means of coping in a harmful and 'self-harming' society. On the one hand, some of these perspectives can provide validation, support, and empathy to individuals. They have also given rise to much-needed challenges to clinical approaches and practices, and have led to the development of ideas for approaches which promote the empowerment of individuals. However, in some user movement approaches we are concerned that there may be a danger of not sufficiently acknowledging the problematic nature of self-injury, and in particular of failing to hear and deal with the enormous individual distress which underlies the self-injury. In responding to self-injury, acceptance and validation are very important; however, it is of primary importance that individuals be accepted for *who they are*, and not because of what they do.

2. The Cross-Cultural and Historical Context of Self-Injury

Self-injury is often seen by others as shocking, frightening, incomprehensible and repulsive. To deliberately injure one's own body is often viewed as something bad or wrong, provoking greater disgust and horror than even violence against other people. In modern Western societies at least, self-mutilation, which might in other contexts be understood as having social or religious significance, is seen as 'mad'. Yet injury to the body (by oneself or by others) is part of a long and universal human tradition, which has had important functions for groups and societies throughout all eras. Body mutilation, pain, and the drawing of blood have had (and continue to have) a range of deep and powerful symbolic meanings in many cultures. In some cases such injuries have been self-inflicted, but with the sanction of the society in which the practice takes place. Also of relevance to our understanding of self-injury are socially-condoned practices whereby injury is inflicted *upon others*. In some instances individuals voluntarily undergo mutilation. In other cases, parents consent to the mutilation of their children, while in some instances representatives of the community as a whole authorize the infliction of physical injury on certain individuals.

In this chapter we will explore some of the ways in which deliberate mutilation of the body has historically been carried out in various societies and the many functions this has served. We will draw many parallels with modern day practices (both in mainstream society as well as in various subcultures) in Western society. We will go on to examine the relationships between such socially-sanctioned customs, and the self-injury which is carried out by people in distress. At this point we wish to mention our indebtedness to Armando Favazza for his groundbreaking and extensive exploration of mutilative practices throughout the world. His gathering together of research in this area (Favazza, 1987) has been invaluable, and in this chapter we quote extensively from examples of practices which he has identified. We go on, however, to develop our analysis of self-mutilation in a way which differs substantially from that of Favazza. Firstly, our emphasis is on functions rather than typologies of self-mutilation. Secondly, we prefer a non-pathologic understanding of self-injury as meaningful and adaptive. While documenting and acknowledging 'the vast array of cultural practices, attitudes and beliefs . . . that form the theater within which self-mutilation is performed' (Favazza, 1987, p. xxiii), he nevertheless viewed self-injury amongst distressed individuals within our own culture as 'deviant', and rooted in 'mental illness', albeit serving a temporarily 'remedial' function for such individuals (pp.191–192). In contrast, we will argue that self-injury has become pathologized as a result of arbitrary and discriminatory distinctions between 'normal' and 'dysfunctional', or comprehensible and mad, features of human behaviour.

Healing and Protection Against Disease

Bodily-mutilation and the drawing of blood have been very important elements of healing practices in many societies. Often it is the body of the sick person which is mutilated, sometimes others' blood and body parts have been used for their healing properties, and in some cases self-mutilation has been central to the development of a healer's powers. Healing has often involved attempts to remove the cause of disease from the body. Favazza (1987, p.33) quotes an example of a Pacific Island practice whereby a person's body would be cut open in order to release vermin which were believed to be present in the body and causing disease. Trephination has been a long-standing and historically extremely widespread practice, whereby the skull is cut or drilled into in order to release compression or evil spirits thought to be causing illness. Mutilation of the body in order to release evil forces, bad 'humours' or blood believed to be implicated in disease has a vast history. Blood-letting (through cutting of veins or leeching) to cure and prevent disease was traditional in Europe from the second century through to the 1800s and even up until the 1920s in some areas. Although such practices may no longer be socially condoned in many countries, related ideas persist. For example, in England recently a young Asian woman died after being beaten systematically and repeatedly by her family in order to 'cure' her of what they believed to be the moral or spiritual basis of her illness.

Other body mutilations which anthropologists have identified as having been carried out in order to cure or protect against illness have included fingertip removal (Virchow, cited in Favazza 1987, pp.106–7), scarification of the flesh (Favazza 1987, pp.128–130) and male infibulation (a practice carried out as recently as the late 19th century in the West, whereby the foreskin of the penis was pierced and a clasp inserted in order to prevent erection and ejaculation. This was thought to be a cure or precaution against conditions such as weakness and epilepsy (Dingwall, cited in Favazza, 1987, pp.158–159).) The practice of excising a woman's clitoris was carried out on a widespread basis in Victorian Britain (and elsewhere) in the belief that this would cure many medical problems supposedly caused by masturbation.

Various cultural practices of mutilation and self-mutilation have been carried out with the aim of ridding the body of evil substances, in order to promote health and strength and avoid sickness. Often such practices are associated with fear of women's menstrual blood, which is seen as malignant and dangerous. Certain tribes in areas of Papua New Guinea practice nasal, tongue and penis mutilation amongst men, inducing heavy bleeding which they believe will rid the man's body of blood from his mother's womb. The practice is referred to as male menstruation, with the implication that men envy women's natural monthly cycle (Hogbin and others, cited in Favazza, 1987, p.95.)

The use of others' blood in the curing of disease has a long history. The blood of gladiators was reported by Pliny to be drunk to cure epilepsy, and the belief that blood drawn from those who have died violently could cure epilepsy persisted into the 19th century. Bathing in blood (usually that of young children) was thought to be a cure for leprosy. The mutilated body parts of saints and martyrs have also long been believed to have miraculous healing properties.

Self-mutilation, as well as starvation and privation of various kinds, have been considered essential means of developing the powers of healers in many cultures. Shamen from various societies undergo initiatory periods involving such procedures as torturing and mutilating their own bodies, walking on hot coals, having their torsos pierced with rods and so on (Favazza, 1987, pp.26–27). Wisdom and enlightenment are also thought to be developed through visions involving their own deaths, dismemberment and reconstitution. In some cultures, healing practices have involved self-injury on the part of the healer; for example the Moroccan Hamadsha brotherhood slash their heads in order to calm the spirits believed responsible for sickness (Favazza, 1987, p.67). In Europe in the Middle Ages, groups of priests flagellated themselves until they bled, in a holy ritual believed to protect communities from plague.

What relationship, if any, do such mutilative practices have to modern day treatment of disease in Western culture? Western medicine, unlike some other medical traditions, gives great prominence to surgery. Surgery, of course, involves mutilation, the removal of parts of the body, and blood transfusion, all of which are regarded as highly acceptable, normal and necessary by society. Evidence that surgery is not always founded purely on scientific principle and necessity can be found in the enormous variations in rates for some surgery between countries with similar disease rates and medical resources. Surgery is more fashionable and in greater demand in some countries (particularly the USA) than in others, and some surgery is arguably of dubious value and necessity. It is also conducted in the context of powerful and precise rituals, by surgeons whose status and mystery in society is equivalent to that of shamen in other cultures.

Most services dealing with individuals' emotional distress, viewed in the Western medical tradition as 'mental illness', involve treatments to the body. The emphasis on physical interventions confirms the idea that we must rely on immediate physical interventions to deal with emotional pain. This same idea is central to self-injury, since many people who self-injure do so in order to provide short-term relief for overwhelming distress. The message which people who self-injure may well be receiving from mental health services is that they are correct in seeking an immediate physical solution to their distress, although psychiatry's interventions are better (or at least more authoritative and socially sanctioned) than their own. Whilst the most common treatments nowadays involve drugs, the irony of treating patients with electric shocks or brain surgery can scarcely be lost on those whose self-injury is seen as a pathological behaviour to be extinguished.

Throughout human history, beliefs and practices concerning healing have involved various kinds of mutilation to the bodies of those who are sick, or to those from whom healing is sought. Perhaps this tradition is reflected in the actions of those who seek to heal themselves of their own mental distress through self-injury.

Spiritual Advancement, Enlightenment and Wisdom

It was seen in the discussion of healing that the development of healing powers amongst shamen goes alongside enlightenment and wisdom, which are developed through privation and self-torture. Similar beliefs and practices are found in other communities, such as Tibetan Tantrics, who achieve enlightenment through visions of horrible mutilation (Favazza, 1987, p.10). For the Moroccan Hamadsha brotherhood, self-mutilation (and ecstatic dancing) are believed to lead to union with spirits as well as the curing of ailments. Native American Plains Indians go through an ordeal involving dancing while attached to a pole with thongs and skewers through their flesh. Enduring this ordeal indicates that the dancer is pure in heart, and his reward (which benefits the whole tribe) is to receive a vision making clear the meaning and course of life (Favazza, 1987, p.11).

Similar traditions, in which suffering and sacrifice are believed to lead to a relationship with the sacred, have existed in most cultures and religions. In Hindu belief we see the importance of self-mutilation in the story of Siva, the son of Brahma the Creator, who castrated himself rather than create imperfect beings. Statues of his severed penis or lingam are sacred symbolic objects, having importance akin to the cross in Christianity. Hindu and Islamic asceticism involve physical privation and suffering as a means of separating from the flesh and the worldly in order to achieve spiritual advancement. Shiite Moslems re-enact the deaths of revered martyrs during annual passion plays, inflicting wounds upon their own bodies.

In the Judaeo-Christian tradition, suffering, martyrdom and the endurance of torture were long associated with piety, devotion to God and sainthood. (Parallels between modern-day self-mutilation amongst depressed individuals and early Christian martyrdom have been proposed by Bradford (1990).) Notions of sacrifice and martyrdom are expressed dramatically in the Old Testament story of Abraham, who was willing to kill his own son, Isaac, at God's command. Saints and martyrs have been revered for their willingness to suffer torture and to die for their faith. In early Christian times some priests adopted the practice of self-castration (thought to achieve purity and holiness) which had originated with the Cybele cult in Asia Minor. Self-castration continued to be practised in some Christian and Orthodox sects into the 19th and 20th centuries (Favazza, 1987, pp.147ff). To this day, some devout Christians (particularly Catholics) believe that the appearance of stigmata (marks or wounds imitating those of Christ) on a person's body are a miraculous indication of great piety and approval by God.

Ideas concerning spiritual progress are often associated with chastity, purity, and defence against (or punishment for) the 'sins of the flesh'. Both socially-sanctioned mutilation and the self-injury carried out by individuals in distress often involve notions of punishment, atonement and cleansing, followed by redemption and salvation.

Punishment, salvation and redemption

Mutilative practices associated with punishment, atonement, cleansing, purity and redemption have been extremely widespread throughout history in most cultures. This theme is found in the Old Testament and in Judaic tradition, and permeates Christianity, where the central belief is that Christ gave Himself up to be flogged and crucified, in order to redeem the sins of humanity. Images of Christ's battered and crippled body, hanging from nails and bleeding from His pierced side and His thorn-crowned head are to be found in many churches, art galleries and homes. During Holy Communion congregations drink red wine and eat wafers, symbolizing Christ's blood and flesh, in order to commemorate Christ's sacrifice and to achieve 'communion' with Him. (While in some traditions the wine and bread are seen as purely symbolic, the dogma of transubstantiation holds that they actually become Christ's blood and flesh.)

The Christian scriptures are full of references to the necessity for the shedding of blood and mortification or mutilation of the body in order to avoid or atone for sin.

'According to the law almost everything is purified by the blood, and without the shedding of blood there is no forgiveness.'
(Hebrews 9:22)

'If your hand or foot is your undoing, cut it off and throw it from you! Better to enter life maimed or crippled than be thrown with two hands or two feet into the endless fire. If your eye is your downfall, gouge it out and cast it from you! Better to enter life with one eye than be thrown with both into Gehenna.'
(Matthew 18:7–9)

The suffering of Christian saints was often a means of atonement and purification, or of maintaining chastity to avoid sin. St Lucy, for example, had consecrated her chastity to God, and underwent torture rather than comply with a sentence of prostitution. Legends about St Lucy hold that she gouged out her own eyes to prevent a young man from sexually desiring her. (Eye-mutilation and blinding have often been endorsed as a punishment for lust. The most familiar literary example of this, other than in religious texts, is the story of Oedipus Rex, who gouged out his eyes on discovering that he had killed his father and had had intercourse with his mother.) The catalogue of self-mortification and mutilation undergone by penitent followers of Christ is huge. This includes self-flagellation, carried out by saints such as St Francis and St Dominic, whose example was followed for hundreds of years by monks, nuns, priests and their congregations throughout Europe. It is only fairly recently that some religious orders have abandoned the practice, and in some parts of the world, public self-flagellation is still practised at Easter (Favazza, 1987, pp.40 ff). Castration also has a long history as a form of punishment, having been adopted by some Christians but originating thousands of years before in Chinese, Egyptian and Babylonian cultures where it was used to punish adultery and sexual crimes. Modern-day Christian pilgrims such as those who annually visit the shrine on a rocky island in Loch Deargh in Ireland continue to undergo pain as part of a ritual of atonement and devotion.

Mortification of the body is not confined to Christian and Judaic tradition. Followers of Islam have also sought to punish and atone for sin through physical suffering and mutilation. Sufis, for example, practise the wearing of uncomfortable, coarse clothing as a penance, while some Shiites flagellate themselves en masse during festivals.

Of course the notion that wrongdoing should be punished and in some way redeemed through inflicting pain and injury on the body is not restricted to religion. Punishment of criminals in most societies has often involved physical chastisement such as flogging, amputation of limbs and tongues, castration, branding and of course execution. Practices such as these persist in various cultures, while even in countries such as Britain where physical punishment has been replaced by imprisonment, many people still support the idea of 'bringing back the birch' or reinstating capital punishment. Discipline of children still involves physical punishment in many homes, and is lawful in most countries. It is significant that physical pain and injury or privation are often seen not just as a means of punishing the offender and deterring them and others from the offending behaviour. There is also the notion that through punishment can be atonement. Like the sinner who can do penance and make his peace with God, the criminal can 'pay his debt to society'. The child's wrongdoing can be forgiven and forgotten.

As will be seen in *Chapter 4*, the idea that wrongdoing deserves, and can be atoned for through, physical punishment is highly significant for our understanding of self-injury amongst individuals in emotional distress. Many people who self-injure do so at least partly as a means of relieving feelings of guilt, shame, 'badness' or contamination. Often such feelings have arisen as a result of childhood abuse, for which the person has blamed herself (and has often been blamed by the perpetrators). Like Oedipus and some martyrs or saints, they may punish their own bodies in an attempt to atone or purify themselves following incest or sexual abuse. Like the child for whom punishment, however painful, at least brings a welcome end to parental disapproval, someone who self-injures may be able to forgive themselves and feel less unacceptable and undeserving for a while. It is clear that in deciding to do so they are drawing not on some deviant and idiosyncratic idea born of their individual pathology, but on profound traditions of human belief and religious and social practice.

Community, Identity and Status

Mutilation of the body is often associated with community identification and loyalty, initiation and rites of passage. Community membership has been signified in different cultures by practices as diverse as cutting off fingers, scarification and circumcision. Many people will be familiar with the idea of sealing a pact or swearing loyalty through an exchange of blood, and the phrase 'blood brothers' is known to most of us, indicating that blood can be a powerful symbol of unity and loyalty. An example of the power of blood as a symbol of initiation is the continuing practice in foxhunting circles of 'blooding' the face of those new to the hunt with the tail of the dismembered fox.

Some of the most dramatic and powerful mutilative practices carried out around the world have been associated with initiation into adulthood. The initiation of boys has often been described in this context, however, one of the most widespread, and, in our opinion, the most brutal, of such practices is that of circumcision of young girls. The nasal, tongue and penis mutilations carried out in New Guinea and referred to earlier also form part of the initiation of boys into manhood. Boys of the Awa tribe from that region undergo rituals in preparation for manhood which involve beating, induced vomiting, being stung with nettles, nasal haemorrhaging and cutting of the penis (Newman and Boyd, cited in Favazza, 1987, p.98). Young Awa women also go through ritual nose-bleeding at the time of betrothal. Amongst indigenous Australian people, male initiation rites involve many physical ordeals, including the knocking out of teeth, nose-piercing, circumcision, walking on fire and subincision of the penis (cutting open the penis from underneath, often laying open the urethra). South American Guyaki boys have their lips pierced and their bodies cut to induce patterns of scarring, whilst among the Motu of New Guinea different areas of girls' bodies are tattooed to mark their passage through various life stages (Favazza, 1987, pp.125–129).

Male circumcision is an extremely widespread practice which continues in the West, and which may have many functions, including identification with the community and its beliefs. Tattooing and body piercing are also familiar modern-day Western practices which may indicate identification with certain social groups, such as sailors, the gay community and other sub-cultures. An example of this within the UK is 'borstal marks' – tattoos made upon themselves and each other by inmates of young offenders' institutions.

Social status may also be indicated by mutilation and marking of the body. Scarification and tattooing have been widely used to communicate information about individuals' status; for example, the intricate Polynesian tattooing and scarification in Cameroon which each indicate high social rank. Low rank and outcast status have also been indicated by tattooing, for example the marking of numbers on concentration camp victims, and the tattooing of 'D' on the wrists of Army deserters in 19th century Britain.

It seems that the idea of self-mutilation to demonstrate community identification and status, although not generally sanctioned in most Western countries, emerges powerfully in certain institutional settings. Self-injury is particularly prevalent in prisons, special hospitals and secure settings, as well as in certain residential settings such as children's homes, hostels for homeless people, and so on. There may be many reasons for this, including individual trauma and distress and environmental factors (these will be explored further in subsequent chapters). However, one factor seems to be that self-mutilation forms part of the culture of the inmate or resident group. Such behaviour may then be a means of demonstrating belonging and solidarity with the group and resistance to those in authority, while the severity of self-injury carried out may sometimes contribute to the status of the individual within the group.

Order and Safety

Often linked to community identification are practices which promote social order, solidarity and a sense of safety and control over destiny. The Ivory Coast Abidji tribe, for example, holds a New Year festival preceded by meetings to discuss and reconcile disagreements and divisions. During the festival there is dancing and drumming, bad spirits are driven away and good spirits invoked, which guide some individuals to slash their own abdomens. The public self-mutilation and subsequent healing of wounds seems to serve the function of demonstrating the healing of social divisions (Favazza, 1987, pp.13 and 23).

The Nigerian Tiv mutilate themselves to make patterns of scarring. Amongst the many social functions this fulfils is believed to be that of representing and ensuring the social order and the continuity of life. Similarly, the initiatory mutilation of Guyaki boys described earlier seems to serve the additional function of preserving order and safety. The tribe believe that a supernatural blue jaguar periodically appears to destroy the universe. The splitting of skin and flesh mirrors the ritual splitting of the earth with axes which the tribe carries out to impose order, and prevent the Earth's destruction by the jaguar.

Many creation myths throughout the world are based on the theme of a deity or being who was sacrificed and mutilated to create the universe and the social order. Such myths are found in many sacred texts; in India, the Rigveda, in Iran, the Greater Bundahisn, and in Scandinavia, the Prose Edda, each of which tell how the world and society were created from the parts and fluids of dismembered bodies of gods, giants and animals. In China, the universe was believed to be born of the mutilation of a giant, P'an-ku. Within the Bible the same theme can be seen in the story of Adam and Eve, where woman was created from the rib taken from the side of Adam. In many communities such myths are traditionally re-enacted in rituals which symbolize the transformation of chaos, sacrifice, suffering and terror into order and security. In Christianity, the most important religious festivals – those celebrating the birth of a 'saviour' and his crucifixion and resurrection – reflect similar themes. Through the mutilation and sacrifice of a deity the world is rescued from sin and the 'forces of darkness', and a new and benevolent order is created.

Suffering and sacrifice have had important functions in the preservation of social order and safety in many cultures. The sacrifice of a human or animal may be carried out to propitiate and obtain favour from powerful and wrathful deities. Other theories hold that sacrifice keeps the gods alive or ensures communion between deities and humans. Girard (1977) suggests that sacrifice provides a means of focusing community tension and conflict onto one victim, thus preserving social harmony and protecting the community from its own violence. (Girard points out that in societies practising human sacrifice, victims have tended to be those not valued or integrated into the community, such as prisoners of war, slaves and disabled people.) Modern parallels can be seen in the scapegoating of certain social groups. In Britain and other Western countries, for example, ethnic minorities are for some a convenient target to blame for problems such as unemployment and lack of public housing. This focuses dissatisfaction and dissent onto a small and relatively powerless group, rather than on the society as a whole and its government. This scapegoating is expressed in racist attacks on Black people which (like the beating-up of gay men and lesbians) could be seen as a modern form of 'sacrifice'

We concur with Favazza (1987, p.25), who suggests that self-injury amongst individuals in distress (described by him as 'mentally ill') may serve similar functions of averting chaos (in this case of a personal, individual nature), and establishing a new and peaceful, if temporary, order. Perhaps we can understand self-injury partly in terms of the widespread human impulse to find a focus for and means of overcoming fear, conflict, powerlessness and distress. The individual 'scapegoats' a part of their own body, which is hurt (sacrificed) to provide a manageable focus and means of expression for their own internal chaos. A sense of control is achieved. The physical healing which follows may symbolize the psychic healing for which the person longs.

Such actions may also serve social functions for the family or community to which the distressed individual belongs. Distress is held by an individual, who is seen as 'ill', thus relieving the family or community from the necessity of acknowledging its own difficulties. The distress is in part expressed by the individual's self-injury, yet its nature and origins remain hidden. Self-injury on the part of the person may be followed by rejection (which allows the group to continue to disown the distress) or by demonstrations of concern and caring, which restore harmony and well-being. Help may be drawn to the individual, but without the real problems of the family or community being exposed. Conflict within the group may also be focused on the 'difficult' individual. As we saw in *Chapter 1*, an example of this is seen in clinical settings where patients' self-injury has been reported to escalate in response to conflict amongst staff teams (Aldridge, 1988) In this way, individuals' self-injury may act as a kind of safety-valve for problems and feelings which are experienced as threatening to a group of people.

Power and Strength

Many mutilative and self-injurious practices have served to demonstrate power, dominance, strength or endurance. Trophies providing evidence of victory in battle have included the heads, noses and scalps of the vanquished, while the taking of blood or of body parts ('an eye for an eye, a tooth for a tooth') has satisfied the need to restore honour. Mutilation and marking of the body connected with strength and power are also often associated with masculinity. In the cultures mentioned earlier which practise nose- and penis-mutilation and bleeding, one purpose is to rid the male body of 'femaleness' and to instil strength and bravado. Amongst the Kagoro in Papua New Guinea, teenage boys endure beatings and painful skin-cutting to form patterns of scars reminiscent of reptile markings. These ordeals (together with practices such as forcing the boys to witness the clubbing to death of their pets) are believed to lead to their rebirth as men, capable of greater strength and endurance (Jilek and Jilek-Aall, 1978, cited in Favazza, 1987, p.130).

In modern Western societies, a form of body 'mutilation' which has frequently been used to demonstrate physical strength and aggressiveness is tattooing. Scars on the bodies of those who have taken part in war, or in some social groups, a fight, have also been seen as a sign of strength and courage and a source of pride. A number of modern-day sports, such as boxing and martial arts reflect similar notions of proving strength by withstanding and inflicting injuries to the body.

Amongst people who injure themselves in response to their own emotional suffering (particularly where this has arisen due to abuse), scarring can similarly be felt to be important as a means of symbolizing what the person has suffered. Scars may provide 'evidence' to the person themselves that they can endure and survive experiences (and resulting feelings) which seem unendurable. An individual may also believe (or hope) that her injuries and scars will communicate to others what she has suffered.

Beauty and Desirability

Many mutilative practices have been (and still are) carried out in order to achieve notions of beauty and desirability (often together with femininity and masculinity). The idea that the human body, especially that of women, requires modification to be beautiful or even acceptable seems to have been universal throughout human history.

Moulding of the head (often from infancy) to achieve a desired shape has been a widespread practice, being carried out in Ancient Egypt and Greece, through to the 19th century in Holland and France. In some societies, the nose has been reshaped; for example, Polynesian people used to break and flatten their noses. In the West, similarly, the nose is often the focus of attention, with cosmetic surgery being undergone to produce what is perceived to be a more attractive shape or size.

Other practices thought to enhance the attractiveness of the body have included earlobe and neck stretching, tooth-filing, scarification, tattooing and footbinding. Footbinding, a process whereby the feet of Chinese girls and women were crippled and deformed to prevent their growth, was inflicted on millions over hundreds of years. The result was apparently extremely attractive and desirable to men.

In the West many normal practices which in fact involve mutilation of the body are accepted as means of becoming more beautiful and desirable. These include various forms of cosmetic surgery to the face and body, as well as practices such as jaw-wiring and stomach-stapling to aid slimming. Hair is removed through plucking, shaving, waxing or electrolysis. It is not many years ago since women tied themselves into tight corsets, breaking ribs and damaging internal organs in order to achieve slim waists (the modern equivalent would be harmful dieting practices), and many still deform their feet and hurt their backs by wearing fashionable high-heeled or pointed shoes. Piercing of various parts of the body has become increasingly fashionable for aesthetic reasons. Black people in the West as well as throughout Africa bleach their skin, causing harm to themselves in order to become a more 'desirable' pale colour, while white people risk burning and skin cancer through their efforts to develop a tan.

As we will discuss further in *Chapter 3*, there is an important relationship between self-injury, and ideas and practices which involve injuring or changing the body to achieve 'beauty'. Individuals, particularly women and Black people, learn that their bodies are not 'good enough' as they are, and that it is normal and desirable that they should modify, hurt and mutilate the body to make it more acceptable and attractive. A distressed individual who feels that she herself (or her feelings, thoughts and experiences) is unacceptable and unwanted may draw on this well-established idea that she can make herself acceptable through modifying her own body. For some people, such ideas are translated into self-starvation or other harmful eating behaviours, for others into self-injury. This is not to suggest that such an individual believes simplistically that mutilation will make her more attractive. A more complex process translates her desire for relief from feelings of 'badness' and unacceptability into the notion that she must physically alter herself in order to become 'acceptable'.

Self-Mutilation and Mourning

In a number of cultures, socially-sanctioned mutilation has been associated with bereavement and mourning. In New Guinea the young women of the Dugum Dani tribe have fingers chopped off as a sacrifice at the funerals of male relatives (Gardner and Heider, 1968, cited in Favazza, 1987, p.106). Members of the Native American Crow tribe would cut off fingers and hair and slash their bodies in mourning the death of a warrior (Favazza, 1987, p.108). Amongst Sandwich Islanders there has been a practice of knocking out teeth in mourning and propitiation for the death of a community leader (Favazza, 1987, p.101). One of the most extreme practices concerned with bereavement was the Indian practice of suttee, where women threw themselves (or were thrown) onto their husbands' funeral pyres. This practice continued for over 500 years. Less drastic practices associated with grief which are still seen in various societies include pulling out one's hair and beating one's breast or head.

These practices seem to serve a variety of functions, sometimes providing an outlet for the extreme pain of grief, at other times serving to mark the significance of the loss. Individuals who self-injure in response to emotional distress may be seeking to fulfil similar functions associated with loss and grief. It will be seen in *Chapter 4* that self-injury sometimes follows bereavement (often in childhood), traumatic separation or loss of an important relationship. Self-injury is also frequently associated with abuse or maltreatment, which involve important forms of loss and can give rise to powerful feelings of grief.

Social Control and the Oppression of Women and Other Groups

It was noted earlier that the punishment of offenders as well as of children has frequently involved physical pain and injury. These serve as a means of social control, and physical punishment and mutilation have been used in various societies over the centuries to control not only criminals but also others who threatened the power of ruling groups. Familiar examples from various countries include political dissidents and activists, trade unionists, civil rights campaigners and peace protesters.

Many brutal practices have been carried out around the world to control and subdue women, as well as oppressed ethnic groups, homosexuals and so on. The practice of suttee referred to earlier (and now illegal) seems to have been to some extent replaced by dowry deaths, where some young Asian brides, whose dowry is felt to be insufficient by the husband's family, burn themselves (or are burned) to death. The burning and torture of women has of course a very long history in Europe, where women suspected of any 'subversion' (often in fact healers) were burned as witches.

Mutilative practices endured by girls and women have included footbinding, mentioned earlier, which functioned not only to make women more 'desirable' but also to control them, since they literally could not walk away from their husbands' demands. In many African countries genital mutilation of millions of girls continues to this day, and is carried out to ensure that women do not have sex with anyone other than their husbands. This practice can be said to be particularly self-mutilative in that it is sanctioned and carried out by women against women. In Britain, the practice of clitorodectomy was similarly carried out to control women's sexuality, and it is instructive to note that the operation is still lawful in Britain, and is sometimes carried out by surgeons at the request of visitors to the country. And whilst the beating of wives by their husbands is no longer sanctioned by law, the battle to persuade the police and the community to fully recognize and prevent domestic violence is still not over. As will be seen in the next chapter, it is in such a context that the greater prevalence of self-injury amongst women must be understood.

Implications for the Understanding of Individuals who Self-Injure

Having examined a range of mutilative practices and their functions from many cultures, it is possible to draw some conclusions as to their relevance to the understanding of self-injury carried out by people in distress. We need to understand this in terms of the functions of self-injury both for individuals, and for the community and society within which they live.

It seems to be a universal feature of human societies that certain social functions are served by the infliction of pain, modification, mutilation or marking upon the body. In many cases such functions are extremely important and the associated mutilation, scarring, or bleeding assume profound psychological and social significance. The power and significance of the body and of what may be done by and to it are known, at least at an unconscious level, by all of us. We are aware of such traditions through our language, reflected in such terms as 'getting one's pound of flesh', 'being bled dry', 'tearing one's hair out', and so on. We may not all have read significant passages of sacred texts or heard of specific practices in various societies, but we are all immersed in the cultural and historic traditions in which body mutilation has played such important roles.

Individuals in distress draw on the whole repertoire of human behaviour in their search for ways of relieving and resolving their difficulties. Some of the functions which mutilation has traditionally fulfilled are precisely those which a person in mental pain might seek, for example: healing; the restoration of order, familiarity and safety; social acceptance, community and harmony; a means of expressing loss and grief; release from guilt; a sense of power and control, and so on. The many functions which self-injury may serve for the distressed individual and those around them will be explored in detail in *Chapter 4*. For now, the fundamental point to be made is that self-mutilation reflects deeply-rooted, widespread beliefs and traditions concerning the efficacy and power of what is done to the body in the expression of profoundly important human concerns.

At the same time, the individual who self-injures needs to be understood within the context of their community, for which self-injury amongst some members may fulfil certain functions. We suggested that self-injury may perform a function of acting out, yet at the same time containing, the distress and pathology of the society in which it occurs. In this way it may serve the interests of at least those sections of a society which prefer to say, in effect, 'shut up and cut yourself', than to face up fully to the maltreatment and oppression of many of the society's members. The distress of those concerned is individualized, pathologized, and 'treated', rather than being laid at the door of the social institutions in which it arises.

We saw also that sacrifice and scapegoating may serve important social functions in focusing community tension onto individual victims, thus preserving overall social harmony. It is interesting to note that those frequently 'selected' as the focus (whether this involves death, beating up, incarceration or more subtle forms of oppression) are often those amongst whom self-injury is also more common. Gay men and women, physically and learning disabled people, prisoners and those in mental distress, for example, are all more likely to be scapegoated, ostracized, abused and oppressed in various ways by others, as well as to injure themselves. It is as if they have themselves taken on the role of 'sacrificial victim' which the community has ascribed them, acting this out on their bodies. The self-injury then 'confirms' their status as weird, sick, bad or mad, and thus less worthy of full, equal consideration and participation in the community. The society thus has scapegoats who can conveniently be seen as 'deserving' of blame and oppression, by virtue of their deviant behaviour.

Cultural values are represented in the body. For example, women's bodies, faces and voices frequently conform to the values and ideas of society concerning acceptable characteristics and behaviour for women. Similarly, representations of apparent aggressiveness, such as scarring, may be seen as acceptable in men but not so in women. (If, however, a man goes so far as to, say, castrate himself, then this will be in opposition to cultural values concerning men's 'virility' and will usually be interpreted as indicative of madness.)

At the same time, the body can be seen as an *active* agent as well as a passive recipient and reflection of cultural values (Csordas, 1994). In this more active role, the body registers and expresses meaning. Self-injury can often have a function for the individual of recording history: *'This is what happened to me, this is how much I hurt'*. In our view, self-injury may also serve a similar function for society. It marks a collective (as well as an individual) experience in a way that draws in those that come across it, and may bridge the empathic gap between knowing and not knowing about what happens to people and how it affects them. In effect, the self-injury 'speaks' about a social experience of which the society would otherwise remain unaware. Anthropological historian Paul Connerton, in his book *How Societies Remember* (1989), makes the following related point:

' . . . mental enslavement begins when memory is taken away. When a large power wants to deprive a small country of its national consciousness it uses the method of organised forgetting . . . or organised oblivion. Contemporary writers are proscribed, historians are dismissed from their posts, and the people who lose their jobs become silenced and forgotten. What is horrifying is not only the loss of human dignity but the fear that there may remain nobody who could properly bear witness to the past . . . . . . the struggle of citizens against state power is the struggle of their memory against forced forgetting . . . and some make it their aim not only to SURVIVE but to REMEMBER . . . and bear witness as writers of oppositional histories.
(p.14)

We concur with Connerton's view that people will do whatever they can, consciously or unconsciously, to record history, and that in doing so they give meaning not only to their own experience but to that of their society at that point in time. For some (such as those in both actual and domestic prisons), self-injury is one way of recording and representing social and political realities by whatever means society allows.

For those working in 'helping' roles with people who self-injure, the understanding of self-injury which this chapter has proposed has a number of implications, as follows:

1. **Normalization:** rather than being a completely alien, incomprehensible and deviant act, self-injury can be seen as a 'normal' and comprehensible behaviour, to the extent that it follows widespread and powerful human traditions. This understanding can be reassuring to practitioners and reduce the likelihood of panic, overreaction, self-blame and punitive responses on their part. Sharing this understanding of self-mutilation as part of the range of normal human behaviour can also help to relieve some of the distressing shame and fear which are often felt by individuals who self-injure.

2. **Understanding** the significance and functions of body-mutilation in various societies may provide important insights into the meanings and functions of self-injury for an individual in distress. Such insights can help practitioners to counter the simplistic and pathologizing explanations of self-injury which are often prevalent in services. These explanations can be replaced by a more rigorous and in-depth understanding of the complex meanings and purposes self-injury may have for individuals.

3. **Recognition** that the individual's self-injury may serve functions for their family, community and society may lead practitioners and their clients to a better understanding of the behaviour and, furthermore, of what may need to be done if the individual is to be able to stop injuring themselves. For example, an individual whose self-injury is expressing yet containing the dissatisfaction and conflict within a family or institution may be subject to subtle yet powerful pressures *not* to stop hurting themselves. The relevance of the circumstances and relationships within the community concerned may need to be acknowledged openly and perhaps action taken to deal with common issues, before the individual will be free to choose whether or not to give up self-injury.

4. **Acknowledgement** of the powerful meanings which self-injury may carry (and of the enormous distress which the individual may be seeking to alleviate) also provide an essential basis for more compassionate, patient and effective therapeutic work with individuals.

3. Self-Injury and Social Forces

Individual experience and circumstances may *underlie* the distress which gives rise to self-injury, but social relations *shape* such experience. The nature of social relations is that some groups have power over others. On a global scale, the Northern hemisphere has power over the Southern. White has power over Black, men have power over women and the rich have power over the poor. Such power relations can be personalized in the family, where women may be oppressed by men, and children may be maltreated by the adults who have power over them. Social factors are reflected in individuals' views of themselves and their own bodies. They influence their relationships with other people. Social and political realities also affect the availability to individuals of material and environmental support, which may make them more or less likely to need to turn to self-injury as a means of coping and expression. The 'language' of injury, then, may be a means by which some individuals 'speak' about what are social and political, as well as personal, experiences. If we are to fully understand and work effectively with people who self-injure, we need to address the contribution of social and political factors to their situation and to the forces which drive them to express themselves by hurting their own bodies.

Clues to the role of social forces in the phenomenology of self-injury may be given by discrepancies in incidence or nature of self-injury between various social groups. In the absence of large-scale epidemiological research, it is difficult to make accurate statements about the occurrence of self-injury within all different groups. Most authors report higher rates amongst women than amongst men (estimates of the ratio varying from 2:1 to 20:1; see, for example, Cross, 1993; Pao, 1969; Favazza, 1989; Simpson, 1976). Clinical and anecdotal evidence seems to suggest that the incidence of self-injury also varies according to such factors as race, sexuality and disability. In this chapter we examine the role of gender, race, disability and sexuality as well as age and class in the phenomenology of self-injury.

Gender Issues and Self-Injury

Women and self-injury

Many authors have noted that self-injury is more common amongst women than men (see earlier references). In our experience there are also some differences in the *nature* of self-injury carried out by men and women. Although men self-injure less commonly, where they do so it seems that the wounds they cause are often more severe than those that women typically inflict upon themselves (this finding was also noted by Pao, 1969).

If there are such differences between women and men, it suggests that there must be gender-specific issues which contribute to the causes of self-injury. Several theories have been suggested as to the nature of these issues. Some focus on the possible significance of anatomical differences between men and women (for example, Cross, 1993), while others concentrate on the effects of gender socialization on boys and girls (for example, Burstow, 1992). It is likely that in practice these factors are intimately intertwined.

Many women are embattled with their bodies. Most feel dissatisfied with their body shape, size and so on. They feel alienated from their own bodies, which seem mysterious, frightening, and out of control. Cross (1993) suggests that the roots of these feelings lie in the nature of women's sexual anatomy, with the differences between girls' and boys' experience of their bodies starting in infancy and young childhood. Little girls do not become as familiar with their genitals as do boys, since these are not so obvious nor so readily accessible, being partly internal. They do not regularly touch themselves in order to urinate, as do boys. Girls explore themselves and masturbate far less often and less directly than boys, and therefore find their genitals more of a source of confusion and anxiety than do boys. In puberty, girls' bodies change abruptly and dramatically, as breasts and hips develop and they have suddenly to cope with the messy and often painful experience of menstruation. Adolescent boys experience themselves mainly as becoming far stronger, and there is no parallel with periods for boys, other than spontaneous ejaculation ('wet dreams'), which is pleasurable and often a source of pride.

Later on, girls and women may feel that their bodies are vulnerable to invasion and control by others. For example, a boy's or man's penis may be experienced as a frighteningly intrusive 'other within'. For an adult woman further frightening experiences may follow, as her body is 'taken over' and its functions changed by pregnancy, childbirth and breast-feeding.

Women's reproductive role renders them in some ways more in touch with their bodies than men may be, so the body is a highly significant stage on which emotions and conflicts are played out. Yet some women at least may feel that they do not 'own' their own bodies, which they perceive as ugly, vulnerable, frightening, disgusting and out-of-control. For girls and women who do not manage to negotiate (at least reasonably comfortably) the developmental 'challenges and paradoxes of the body' outlined by Cross, self-injury may become a means of attempting to take ownership of their own bodies, of making them feel more known and under their own control.

Cross' analysis provides useful insights into some ways in which men's and women's differing physical experiences of themselves may be related to self-injury. What needs to be added to the argument, however, is recognition of the social influences which contribute to both sexes' experience of their own bodies, and indeed of themselves. Girls do not, for example, explore themselves less and masturbate more rarely than boys simply because their genitals are less accessible (in fact the clitoris is highly accessible), but because in Western society (as in many other cultures) girls and women are not encouraged to take control of their own sexual pleasure. Social prohibition regarding masturbation and sexual activity is far greater for girls and women than for boys and men, hence the large number of insults available to be applied to women who do pursue their own sexual gratification without concern for their 'reputations': 'slut', 'slag', 'tart', 'whore', and so on. There are no comparable words for men, as terms such as 'stud', 'wolf', and so on have connotations of admiration rather than disapproval. Girls do not proudly compare their genitals or discuss the frequency of their orgasms as boys do, because they have learned that it would be unacceptable for them to do so. They have picked up the message that cultural attitudes towards women's sexual and reproductive organs and functions are highly ambivalent. Their discomfort with menstruation, for example, is due not only to the physical pain and inconvenience involved, but also reflects feelings of shame, embarrassment and self-disgust, engendered by social attitudes (conveyed for example, by advertisers of sanitary towels and tampons) which tell them that menstruation is something embarrassing and dirty, to be kept as 'discreet' and 'hygienic' as possible.

Attitudes to women's bodies, particularly their sexual areas, are contradictory, with many negative overtones. The teaching women receive about their bodies from advertising, magazines and entertainment and often from their families and peers tells them that the female body is something to be controlled and tailored in order to please others. Few girls or women can completely resist the expectation that they should make themselves 'attractive', a word whose implication is that their bodies are there primarily to be looked at and found pleasing to others, rather than to be functional, effective and pleasurable for themselves. Feminine attractiveness includes being deodorized, shaved, plucked, made-up, with the right kind of hair, features, skin and body shape. Women must walk a tightrope between being 'attractive', yet not looking 'tarty', or, in later years, like 'mutton dressed as lamb'. Small wonder that many women feel profoundly dissatisfied with, and alienated from, their own bodies. And from feeling that one's body is alien, and potentially ugly, dirty, smelly, fat and unacceptable unless changed and controlled, it is not a large step to deciding to hurt one's own body, given a sufficient level of unexpressed emotional distress.

The importance given to feminine 'attractiveness' may explain why self-injury seems to be seen as so 'wrong', deviant and upsetting (often more so than other self-destructive behaviours, such as eating disorders). Mutilation of the body is absolutely the opposite of what an idealized woman is supposed to do: to make great efforts to be attractive and perfect. In injuring her own body, a woman spoils the thing which society both values and despises. Perhaps this 'spoiling' expresses not just her self-hatred and despair, but also her protest at the contradictory expectations and perceptions placed upon her, and so contains deliberately proud and angry elements.

Femininity does not only demand physical attractiveness. Little girls soon learn what is acceptable female behaviour, and what will result in them being regarded as greedy, selfish, spoilt, a 'tomboy', or simply not very nice. Amongst the injunctions against 'unfemininity' which have most relevance to self-injury are those which prevent women from expressing their feelings fully and taking control of their own lives. It is not feminine to be angry, to protest forcefully, to stand up for one's own rights, opinions and interests. It is not 'womanly' to assert one's own needs, to insist on following one's own beliefs and concerns. The familiarity of insulting words applied to women who behave in these ways, such as 'castrating', 'domineering', 'demanding', 'pushy' and 'hysterical', indicate the strength of reaction which flouting the demands of femininity can bring. Self-injury is often a means of attempting to feel (and perhaps protest) a degree of control over one's life, and at other times a means of expressing and/or punishing oneself for one's emotional needs. The social prohibitions on women in asserting themselves and their needs actively and verbally are therefore highly significant.

Femininity imposes a whole series of demands and constraints on women's behaviour, many of which are contradictory. It is feminine to be gentle, quiet, passive and nurturing, pleasing others and putting their needs before one's own. Yet it is contemptible to be a 'doormat'. It is womanly to make one's marriage or relationship work, to 'stand by one's man', yet a woman who stays with a violent husband is often seen as only having herself to blame. A 'real woman' is sexually available, submissive and pleasing to men, yet if she is harassed or raped she has 'asked for it'. She should have been more assertive or learned self-defence. A similar contradictory set of demands requires that a woman should not be too intellectual or competent at 'technical' things, yet neither must she be a 'bimbo'.

There are many other ways in which the demands of femininity may contribute to some women's urge to self-injure. Most women nowadays have jobs outside the home and yet still undertake much of the housework, household management, childcare and nursing of sick or elderly family members. Women feed and maintain others, both physically and emotionally, which imposes both physical and psychological burdens. Not only are women's bodies (and energies) required to please and sexually gratify others, they must also be available to nurture and serve other people.

Women do not get paid for their domestic work, which is not adequately valued by society and hence not by themselves nor by the family for whom they work so hard. Often their paid work is similarly underpaid and of lower status than that of men. The outcome for many women is to feel exhausted and further alienated from their own bodily and emotional needs. Starved of the attention, recognition and support which they offer to others, they undervalue and despise themselves. Since they are only doing what women are expected to do, their resentment and dissatisfaction seem unreasonable and are again hidden and turned inwards.

The responsibility which women tend to carry for relationships and the personal, emotional spheres of life, although in some respects carrying the potential for great personal satisfaction, can also be problematic. Where responsibility lies, comes also the potential for blame, and many women blame themselves (and are blamed) for the unhappiness, anger and jealousy of others (especially men), as well as for any abuse they themselves suffer. Self-blame is often a factor at the root of self-injury, and it is something which it is difficult for individual women to escape in the context of a society which expects them to take responsibility for so much.

These many (and contradictory) perceptions and demands place stresses on women which are highly significant for our understanding of those who self-injure. Firstly, to consistently suppress one's own needs and feelings and to continue, unprotesting, to tolerate unfair, unfulfilling or abusive situations is deeply damaging to one's self-esteem and emotional health. Secondly, to be in a situation in which one cannot win, since there are penalties for whichever course of action one takes (that is, to endure one's situation or to refuse to tolerate it), can engender a sense of powerlessness, frustration and despair. Depending on the degree to which an individual woman's needs are flouted and she is exploited or abused, a smaller or larger reservoir of unexpressed resentment, grief and anger is likely to build up. In the absence of safe and culturally sanctioned

41

outlets for these feelings, and aided by her low self-esteem, the woman's feelings are likely to be turned inwards upon herself, sometimes through the medium of self-injury.

Men and self-injury

Whilst the women's movement and feminist psychology have given a voice to the experience of women in relation to self-injury, there is no real parallel to account for men's particular experience. It may be that men's self-injury relates to their social experience in similar and/or different ways from that of women. Whilst more work needs to be done in this area, some relevant issues may be identified.

In contrast to women, boys and men are encouraged and allowed to achieve mastery (and so ownership) over their own bodies and their sexuality. There is little, if any conflict for a boy about the development of an adult male body, with the increased musculature and body hair, the deepened voice and the development of the genitals that this brings. There are not the prohibitions on the development of independence, assertiveness, self-expression and determination that beset women as they grow into adulthood. However, boys and men are affected by certain other expectations which may have relevance for self-injury.

Men are subject to expectations of 'masculinity', which has traditionally been defined as involving size, strength, musculature, a deep voice, ability to withstand pain and so on. Personality traits associated with masculinity include fearlessness, assertiveness and, to some extent, aggression, and a logical rather than emotional approach to life. Men are expected to be successful in certain quite public spheres, such as sport, manual skills, career, income, and ownership of material things such as cars. If they 'fail' in these spheres, for example due to unemployment or illness, men may feel that they have no role or power and may become more vulnerable to depression and emotional difficulties, which of course may possibly lead to self-injury.

Boys and men in Western culture are not traditionally expected to cry, nor to display weakness, fear or vulnerability. It may be that men are also made to feel some alienation from their bodies, because they fail to match an ideal of masculinity (or, increasingly, of 'attractiveness' as this is defined for men). They may attempt to dissociate themselves from any 'weakness' or emotionality which their bodies betray. For some men, self-injury may be in part a way of proving their bravado, strength and endurance. This may contribute to an explanation of the frequently more violent, bloody and public nature of some men's self-injury, such as punching walls, causing large gashes. At the same time, men's bodies are still more private than women's, and there is still less (albeit growing) pressure upon them to be 'beautiful', or to experience or perceive their own bodies as others' or public 'property'. This may be reflected in men's attitude to their own self-injury. In our clinical experience, once they have carried out the act of self-injury, it is over and they do not seem to be as secretive and shameful as women do about it. It can be difficult to engage men in discussion of their self-injury in therapy, since they do not appear to see it as significant as women do.

Because women, rather than men, are seen as the primary custodians of emotional life, men may fail to develop an emotional vocabulary or relationships in which their deep feelings can be expressed. Whilst there are many (more or less) culturally sanctioned ways for men to express anger (such as taking part in or watching aggressive sports, shouting, fast driving), there are few ways in which they are likely to feel comfortable in expressing other emotions, such as sadness or grief. Men tend to confine their expressions of such feelings to their most intimate relationships with women, and to be far less likely than women to have friends in whom they can confide. The loss of a relationship with a female partner is therefore particularly significant. In our experience, where men self-injure they often explain this in terms of the break-up of a relationship or 'betrayal' by a woman. They may be reacting to a sense of their own helplessness in taking care of their own emotional (and physical) needs. Possibly their angry display of their feelings through self-injury is in part a protest against the woman reneging on what they see as her responsibility for looking after *their* feelings.

The relative rarity of self-injury amongst men may be also partly explained by the fact that men make use of certain other coping strategies (many of which are less sanctioned or available to women). They more frequently deal with their most uncomfortable feelings by using means such as drinking, drugs, work, hobbies, sport and so on as an escape. (Self-injury, although it may also serve a function of distracting from emotional pain, is less avoidant since it is so clearly evident of emotions.) Men may also convert their less 'acceptable' feelings into anger, which some express through violence and crime – abuse of others, rather than themselves. Thus they remain powerful rather than vulnerable, active rather than passive. This is entirely consistent with their socialization into a 'masculine' role, while accepting and internalizing painful experiences and punishing oneself is consistent with notions of femininity (Graff and Mallin, 1967).

Men in prisons

It seems significant that men's self-injury is higher within prison populations than in the general population (Toch, 1975). Perhaps men begin to self-injure on entering prison partly because their normal supports and coping strategies are not so available to them. At the same time, they are exposed to a culture of greater violence and 'macho' expression than they may be used to outside prison. A major factor may also be that in prison men experience degrees of powerlessness and lack of control which, in the wider society, are normally more familiar to women. They no longer have the freedom of decision, action and movement which they may normally enjoy. Toch (1975) found that male inmates viewed the prison environment as overpowering, unfair and malevolently arbitrary. For these men, self-mutilation was both a means of coping and an attempt to obtain some influence over aspects of an environment in which they felt powerless.

Men's powerlessness as prison inmates may be exacerbated by sexual objectification, abuse and violence from other inmates. Such occurrences, though frequently reported anecdotally, tend to be largely hidden and unacknowledged within prisons. Here, men are again being subjected to experiences (this time of abuse and subsequent silencing) which are normally more likely to be suffered by women. Self-mutilation may be a means of survival in a dangerous subculture. Injuries may express an individual's distress, but they may also attempt to give a message 'Don't mess with me, I'm tough; look what I have withstood'.

Self-Injury and Age

It seems from our experience of both psychiatric patients and of those contacting crisis support services that while some older people (that is, 50 years +) do injure themselves, most self-injury is carried out by younger individuals. Several authors have reported that the majority of those who self-injure are in their teens, 20s and 30s (Favazza, 1993; Graff and Mallin, 1967). While there have been suggestions that self-injury is increasing in the population as a whole (Walsh and Rosen, 1988), what little available data exists appears to suggest that this increase mainly involves younger people, and that self-injury declines with age for individuals.

Young people may be more vulnerable to self-injury for a number of reasons. Firstly, they may still be living with or dependent upon families who are abusive or who provide insufficient nurture and support. They may be struggling with issues of sexuality (as we shall see later, gay young people are particularly vulnerable), or be experiencing bullying or abuse from peers. They will have had little time or experience to help them to develop mature coping skills or to resolve emotional difficulties caused by the kinds of childhood experiences which frequently underlie self-injury (see *Chapter 4*).

Younger people have often relatively less power over the circumstances of their lives than older people. They may have few choices about such matters as work or accommodation, and little money. At the same time they are likely to be particularly concerned with issues of independence and separation/individuation. In this context, self-injury may be compelling, partly as a means of experiencing some sense of control in their lives, and of asserting some independence and identity. Spandler's (1996) research with a group of young people found that control was frequently an important function of the various forms of self-harm in which they engaged. Self-injury may sometimes also function as a means of belonging and gaining status in certain peer groups. In this connection it is interesting to recall that body mutilation has frequently featured in coming-of-age and initiation rites in many cultures, as we saw in *Chapter 2*.

Isolation and lack of support are common features in the backgrounds of people who self-injure. These factors may affect some young people more than is recognized. Whilst peer relationships are very important to young people, at the same time their relationships may be more transitory and limited than those of older people with established partnerships and families. From our experience of working with young people it is also clear that they may find it difficult to obtain support from older adults, who sometimes view young people's feelings and difficulties as trivial.

The apparent decline of self-injury with age is in some respects surprising, since a number of factors might reasonably be expected to lead to *more* self-injury with increasing age. Older women conform even less to stereotyped expectations of 'beauty' – such as having firm, wrinkle-free flesh and skin – than do most younger women, and so might be expected to feel even more dissatisfied with and alienated from their own bodies. Older people are also less valued in other ways by Western society. Status is largely determined in society by occupation and money, and once past retirement age most people are financially worse off, as well as losing their work role and recognition. They may also become more isolated, as daily contact with colleagues is lost. For women, some status also accrues from being a mother, or of childbearing age and potential, and this is lost with the menopause. It might reasonably be expected then, that advancing age may bring loss of self-esteem and greater alienation, resulting in more self-injury.

The fact that older people seem to self-injure *less* commonly may be attributable to greater emotional maturity. However, it may also be that with advancing age a person is able to shed some of the oppressive role expectations which beset them when younger. Perhaps women are able to leave behind some of the demands of femininity, and no longer feel so pressured to be sexually desirable and available.

Neither do they have to continue to be available for childbearing, and their responsibilities for others' needs are likely to be at least somewhat reduced. After they retire women may also be freed from work roles which often mimic their 'feminine' domestic roles.

It is possible that the shame and stigma associated with self-injury are even more keenly felt by some older people, and that under-reporting of self-injury is even greater in this group. As with young people, the emotional suffering of old people in particular is often not fully recognized, and counselling is rarely offered. Whilst available evidence suggests that self-injury is relatively rarer amongst older people, where it does occur we are concerned that the problem and the distress accompanying it should not be overlooked.

Self-Injury and Issues of Race, Culture and Ethnicity

Whilst there is a body of literature concerning the relationships between factors of race, culture and ethnicity and suicide/para-suicide (for example, Soni Raleigh and Balarajan, 1992; Merrill and Owens, 1986), there is very little evidence as to the significance (if any) of such factors in respect of self-injury specifically. Muluka (1986) noted that 'severe self-destructive behaviour' (by distressed individuals) was rarely reported from the African continent and the Third World. However, he concluded that self-mutilation was probably occurring as commonly in these areas as in Western countries, commenting that 'overall one is impressed more by the similarities across the cultures than any differences' (Muluka, 1986, p.779). There is some evidence that migration may be a factor in self-injury (Simpson and Ng, 1992). People coming new to a country and culture (and possibly not fluent in its first language) may suffer distressing feelings of loss, dislocation and disorientation, and may face practical and financial difficulties, with little social support. There is a need for more research attention to the incidence, nature and implications of self-injury amongst people of different ethnic groups. This is particularly important in the light of what we have seen in *Chapter 2*; that is, when self-mutilation is understood in its fullest socio-cultural context, what appear to be pathological behaviours are revealed to be profoundly meaningful, both to the individual and to their society.

One area of growing concern in the UK is the incidence of self-harming behaviour amongst young Asian women (Soni Raleigh and Balarajan, 1992). Whilst most of the research evidence concerns apparent suicides and suicide attempts, we are also aware through our own work and that of colleagues of a high incidence of self-injury in this group. A number of social factors may account for this.

In their analysis of possible reasons for the high rate of suicide by self-burning in young Asian women, Soni Raleigh and Balarajan draw on a number of studies which suggest that such women are subject to particular pressures following from their roles in Indian society, such as 'Submission and deference to males and elders, arranged marriages, the financial pressures imposed by dowries, and ensuing marital and family conflicts' (p.367). These pressures, they argue, are as powerful for women living in India (amongst whom rates of suicide and attempted suicide are similarly high) as for those of Indian origin living abroad. However, an additional factor which may cause distress for individuals of Asian origin living in Western countries may be the 'straddling' of two, often conflicting, cultures, where aspects of the culture of the home are not reflected in the wider society. Indeed, Soni Raleigh and Balarajan note that young people within immigrant Indian communities are particularly vulnerable to anxiety about 'non-conformist behaviour', since their cultural traditions demand unquestioning compliance with elders. Merrill and Owens (1986) found that a significant number of Asian women living in Birmingham, UK, who had attempted suicide had previously rejected arranged marriages or rebelled against the imposition by their parents of what they felt to be restrictive Asian customs. Many felt that they had to make an impossible choice between being ostracized by their families and community or abandoning their desire for a less restrictive lifestyle. The gulf between the culture of an individual's home and immediate community and that of the wider society may lead to conflict, isolation and alienation, which could have implications for self-injury. For some Asian women there may be a greater likelihood of isolation, as problems tend to be regarded as private within the family to an even greater extent than is the case within white society. This is reflected in the relative under-use of mental heath services by Asian people (Beliappa, 1991).

Racism may affect individuals in a number of ways which may have relevance for self-injury. In Merrill and Owens' (1986) study, three Asian females who had attempted suicide gave racist bullying at school as a reason, while several individuals from various racial/ethnic backgrounds taking part in Arnold's research (1995) felt that experiencing racial harassment, abuse or discrimination had contributed to the distress which led them to injure themselves. The trauma, fear, isolation and alienation which such experiences may lead to could clearly be expected to lead to self-hatred and thus to self-injury for some people. One significant way in which racist attitudes may affect people is in their perceptions of and feelings about themselves and their own bodies. Evidence that many black people are made to feel uncomfortable about certain characteristics of their bodies is provided by practices such as hair straightening, skin bleaching and facial surgery. We discussed how women's propensity to self-injure may be influenced by their experience of their own bodies as ugly, unacceptable and in need of modification, and such factors may similarly influence people from oppressed racial groups.

There is evidence that within mental health services Asian and black Afro-Caribbean people are more likely to be compulsorily admitted to hospital, diagnosed as 'schizophrenic' and treated with anti-psychotic drugs than white people are (McGovern and Cope, 1987; Littlewood and Cross, 1980). They are also less likely to receive counselling or psychotherapy. Those who self-injure are thus given fewer opportunities to translate their expressions of distress from the 'language of the body' into verbal communication. There is a clear need for the provision of more relevant and effective forms of support for people from ethnic minority groups. These include services organized from within communities, staffed by workers familiar with the culture and language of users.

Self-Injury and Class Issues

Little is known about the relationship (if any) of class to self-injury, and it is not our impression that there is a direct link between education/social class and likelihood of self-injury. There may appear from evidence of prison and psychiatric populations to be a preponderance of self-injury amongst working class people, yet since such people are over-represented in these contexts this tells us little. (Self-injury is also far more likely to be detected in hospital and prison settings than when it is carried out by those living and holding down jobs in the community.) Non-statutory support agencies can provide some important information. Voluntary agencies, university counselling services (Robinson, 1996), and independent counsellors and therapists all report that they encounter self-injury amongst middle class people and professionals. There is anecdotal evidence that self-injury (such as arm-slashing) occurs in the upper classes, and support for this view was recently provided in Britain by the Princess of Wales, who acknowledged her own self-injury in a television interview for the BBC's 'Panorama' programme.

Some of the factors which may contribute to an individual's level of distress and thus propensity to self-injure are likely to feature more in the lives of working class than of middle class people. These factors include poor housing and homelessness, unemployment, poverty, educational disadvantage, and low-status, physically demanding work where the individual has little opportunity for self-determination and fulfilment. These in turn are likely to lead to low self-esteem and feelings of powerlessness and alienation. Other factors may include living in a less pleasant environment and fewer opportunities (especially for women) to be mobile and to take part in outside activities, gaining respite from the demands of home and childcare. It may also be the case that traditional expectations of male and female roles persist more powerfully in working class communities.

When they approach services, working class people are less likely than middle class people to be offered psychological explanations for their feelings, or to be offered talking therapies. And they are far less likely than middle class people to be able to pay for private therapy. Any possible predisposition against understanding and dealing with their feelings in psychological and verbal terms is therefore compounded, and the somatic framework (which is reflected in self-injury) is reinforced.

Middle class people may be more subject to such stresses as excessively high expectations (for example, of academic success), a factor which emerged in Arnold's research as sometimes involved in self-injury. Despite a possible general propensity to discuss things more in middle class families, there may be lack of communication about emotional issues in families where 'appearances' and self-control are valued over self-expression and mutual support.

Sexuality and Self-Injury

It has become clear in recent years that rates of self-harm are disproportionately high amongst lesbians and gay men, and particularly amongst younger members of these groups. Here again, most of the research evidence concerns what are described as 'suicide attempts'. A survey carried out for the London Lesbian and Gay Teenage Group found that 20 per cent of respondents reported having attempted suicide *because* of their sexuality (Trenchard and Warren, 1984). However, it seems clear that self-destructive behaviours generally, including self-injury, are more prevalent amongst gay and lesbian people (Davies and Neal, 1996). In Arnold's survey, a number of women reported having self-injured as a response to the conflicts and distress they experienced in connection with their lesbianism.

There are a number of reasons why lesbians and gay men, especially when young, are likely to be particularly vulnerable to impulses to hurt their own bodies. Such people are not immune to the sex-role stereotypes and expectations discussed earlier, yet they are clearly flouting them through their choice of sexual partners. Homosexuality is still not fully accepted as a valid sexual identity, and there is still much discrimination against, and indeed abuse of, gay men and women. Trenchard and Warren's survey

(1984) found that 21 per cent of lesbian and gay young people reported having been beaten up because of their sexuality. It is extremely difficult to consistently maintain one's self-confidence and self-esteem when in a minority which does not conform to social norms, particularly when one's identity and sexual behaviour are frequently seen as alien, ludicrous or disgusting. Such difficulties may be exacerbated for young people, who may have a greater need than adults for identification with, and acceptance by, peers. Young gay men and lesbians can be extremely isolated, especially if living in rural areas. Rothblum (1990, cited in Davies and Neal, 1996) found that isolation promoted self-destructive behaviour amongst young lesbians. Many feel forced to be secretive about their sexuality. Some incur great hostility from their own families if their sexuality becomes known (11 per cent of young people in Trenchard and Warren's survey had been thrown out of their homes). An individual's resulting shame, self-hatred and alienation may be compounded if they experience their sexuality as something outside their own control. These factors can create conditions ripe for self-injury to take place.

Self-Injury Amongst Disabled People

Several researchers have found a strong relationship between serious, chronic childhood illness (effectively giving rise to temporary if not permanent disability) and self-injury in childhood or later life (see, for example, Walsh and Rosen, 1988). We are not aware of any research specifically examining the relationship between physical disability arising in adulthood and self-injury, but it seems reasonable to expect a similar correlation might exist. Certainly illness in adult life was mentioned by some women in Arnold's study as a factor which they felt had led to their self-injury.

It is clear that self-injury is particularly common amongst people with various kinds of learning disability (Winchel and Stanley, 1991). This is often attributed to some organic cause, to lack of stimulation or to communication difficulties (Winchel and Stanley, 1991; Walsh and Rosen, 1988). In our experience, it is far less often recognized that learning disabled people may also self-injure for similar reasons to those attributed to non-learning disabled people. It is only quite recently, for example, that sexual and physical abuse of learning disabled children and adults has begun to be acknowledged. Abuse of physically disabled children and women was similarly 'invisible' for many years (Westcott, 1991; Stimpson and Best, 1991, cited in a report of the Women's Support Project, 1995).

Explanations of self-injury amongst physically sick and disabled children and adolescents have included the concept of body alienation. Several authors have reported that such children often have a distorted and confused body image, perceiving their bodies as separate and alien from themselves (Geist, 1979). This sort of body alienation is suggested by Walsh and Rosen (1988) as being a 'pre-requisite in the preparation of one's body as the target of self-harm'.

It is clearly important to recognize the significance of an individual's physical and psychological experience of their own particular illness or disability and of its treatment. However, disability is also a social experience, which occurs within a particular social context. Hughes (1982) reported that sick and disabled children commonly speak of themselves as being 'ugly, defective and unacceptable'. These comments suggest that the children's feelings of alienation are caused in part by their awareness of social attitudes to the body and to disability, as well as by their physical experience of themselves. In a society where prevailing images of the human body are of youth-fulness, fitness and flawlessness, it is very difficult for a disabled person not to feel unacceptable, 'wrong' or invisible.

Disability also frequently brings social isolation, powerlessness and stigmatization. Most disabled children are still not integrated within mainstream schools, while some are institutionalized. Their educational and social opportunities are therefore often severely restricted. Some disabled people (including many with learning disabilities) spend their whole lives in institutional settings. Many disabled adults are unemployed, as well as being effectively excluded from many social settings by poor access. They are also likely to be disadvantaged financially. Social perceptions and attitudes to disabled people include seeing them as unintelligent and unable to communicate, as being asexual, childlike and dependent, passive and so on.

In such a context, self-injury could have many meanings, ranging from punishing one's own body for not conforming to an acceptable and 'desirable' image, to expressing extreme frustration and anger. Perhaps self-injury serves to provide a sense of control over a recalcitrant body, or over a life which is severely constrained by society's failure to allow disabled people to play a full part in the life of the community. It may also be an attempt to communicate distress, grief and protest at one's situation.

For some disabled people communication is a particularly significant issue which may have relevance to self-injury. Deafness, blindness, cognitive and speech difficulties may result in severe limitations on participation in a community which relies on fast and accurate spoken and written communication. Self-injury may well be an attempt to communicate difficulties and needs, or to protest at one's frustration and isolation where the community does not adequately recognize nor facilitate other forms of communication.

Social Forces and Individual Experience

What is the relationship between the social context in which people may self-injure, and individual experience? The concept of a continuum helps to explain the differences between individuals' experiences and responses. At one end of the continuum social relations are expressed at their most oppressive and violent. This would be the case, for example, in families where women and girls are violently and sexually abused, or in situations where racism is particularly powerful and there is little community support for those victimized. At the other end of the continuum there are conditions where the inequalities and abuses resulting from social relations are least in evidence, and are countered or mitigated by the family or community. An example of this would be a family which nurtures, supports and encourages all its members, and is itself backed up by a supportive community.

People whose experience places them further towards the abusive end of the continuum are more likely to suffer extreme distress and conflict which they attempt to survive through injuring themselves. People at the other end of the continuum, whilst they may still belong to a vulnerable group, are more likely to be protected and nurtured, and to develop sufficient self-support to survive their difficulties without the need for recourse to strategies such as self-injury.

Implications for Working with People who Self-Injure

Recognition of the ways in which social forces may be involved in self-injury has a range of implications for practitioners. We may find ourselves in the position of attempting to find individual solutions to social problems. We can only work with individuals (although we may also have, or be able to help them exert, some influence in wider aspects of their lives). We cannot individually change the sexism, racism, class inequalities and other oppressions which may underpin their experiences and difficulties (although as individuals we may play a part in movements to bring about change). This may be very frustrating, and it can be tempting to pathologize the person who self-injures and blame them for resisting our efforts to help, rather than to live with the limitations and contradictions which the social context of our work imposes.

What practitioners wishing to help people who self-injure can usefully do is to take social factors fully into account in their work. In practice this may mean the following:

1. Being alert to the social contexts of clients' lives, and recognizing how these may contribute to the causes of self-injury. In some cases this will be more obvious: all women live in the context of sexism, all ethnic minorities in the context of racism. Other oppressions may not be so obvious to us unless we provide sensitive opportunities for people to tell us about them. For example, we may not realize that someone is gay, poor or unemployed, that they have been a refugee, or that they have suffered because of a disability which is not obvious. Awareness needs to be supported by education: workers can work far more effectively if they are accurately informed about the experience of people from social groups different from their own.

2. Examining our own attitudes and practice to ensure that we are not furthering (and are preferably *countering*) discrimination and oppression. If we cannot genuinely accept and support someone because of our own prejudices against their sexuality, gender, race or other characteristics, we are not the right person to be working with them.

3. Ensuring that services are appropriate to the needs of people from various social groups. This may involve, for example, enabling clients to choose to see a worker of their own sex or ethnic origin. To be truly accessible to women, services need to recognize and cater for women's childcare responsibilities, and to provide women-only space. There needs to be proper provision for the needs of disabled people, for those whose first language is not English, and so on. In some cases, it may be most appropriate for service providers and purchasers to support the setting up of services organized *within* a community, and staffed by members of that community.

4. Helping our clients to understand their experience and their self-injury in terms of its social as well as individual context, and supporting them in voicing their feelings about this. However, we need to guard against shaming people by insensitively forcing upon them our own perceptions of any social deprivation or oppression to which they may be subject. A helping relationship by its very nature involves inequality, which may be exacerbated by differences between the helper and the client in terms of gender, class, education, income, and so on. It is for the helper to work to minimize the gulf and the power differential between themselves and their clients, in terms of such things as the language they use, the settings in which they see people, and how arrangements are negotiated. It may also be more appropriate to withhold unsolicited comments about a person's possible experiences of oppression, but to be sensitive and supportive to the person's own expressions of these.

5. Encouraging clients, where possible, to take appropriate action to free and empower themselves. This might mean helping them to be more assertive, to be more aware of their rights, or to make contact with support groups.

6. Addressing the real material and social circumstances of a person's life (for example, poor housing, isolation, domestic violence) as well as their internal, psychological experience. If this is not within the scope of our role, we can inform and refer clients to other appropriate agencies.

7. Acknowledging that while we can help an individual to recover from the psychic wounds caused to them, we cannot change the oppressive circumstances in which they are rooted. We also need to recognize that, as someone changes and is less prepared to accept oppressive treatment from others, they may encounter quite a backlash. For example, if someone who has put up with very poor pay and conditions at work begins to speak out, they may feel better about themselves, but they may also lose their job. A young person who can no longer bear living 'in the closet' and tells his parents or friends that he is gay may be ridiculed or ostracized. A woman who stands up to an abusive husband may get beaten up. What practitioners can do is to help people to give themselves more choices, in full awareness of the possible implications of exercising these, and support them in making and living with their choices.

Working in this 'politicized' way is not without problems. On an individual level, practitioners (particularly in statutory settings) may encounter resistance and hostility to working in ways which recognize people's oppression and seek to empower them. This resistance is a reflection of the powerful resistance in society to change in the very social relations which may be at the root of their clients' difficulties.

The groups with most advantage in society have much to lose by allowing inroads into their power. It follows that if people who have previously been quiescent begin to challenge their oppression and demand greater equality, others who benefit from their current position will be extremely threatened and will attempt to restore the status quo, by various means.

The relationship of this to self-injury stems from the functions self-injury may have in allowing an individual to tolerate her situation. For some people at least, self-injury has the functions of expressing anger, frustration, despair and protest. It may also be a way of attempting to gain a sense of control and agency in their lives. Yet an individual's protest and attempts to achieve some control or power in this way may not really be effective. Her anger is visited upon herself and no real challenge or change to the status quo is made. If such people did not self-injure, perhaps they would no longer be able to tolerate their situations. Perhaps their anger and wish for power would no longer be contained, but would be expressed outwardly, at least at the level of the family, the home, the workplace and the community, if not through larger movements for social change.

In the last chapter we saw that self-injury may be functional for society, as well as for the individual. It may not be in the interests of those with privilege and power if people stop injuring themselves and begin to express their dissatisfaction outwardly. Self-injury, like many other behaviours (such as gambling, use of alcohol and drugs, and so on), may in fact serve the interests of those with privilege and power in society, by providing a 'safety valve' for the dissatisfaction of some who are oppressed, and so reducing the potential for real protest and resistance.

Medicine, psychiatry and other health and social welfare institutions reflect societal power relations (and are usually staffed, at least at the higher levels, by representatives of privileged groups, such as white middle class men). Such institutions are in a paradoxical position. They exist to make people better, which with someone who self-injures implies helping them to stop hurting themselves. Yet they and the power structures of the society which they serve may be very threatened if large numbers of hitherto quiescent individuals stop hurting themselves and start directing their anger and resistance outwards at the people and institutions which oppress them.

The 'solution' found to this dilemma is often to individualize and pathologize people's distress. Instead of asking the question, 'What is wrong in our society that makes large numbers of its members in particular groups hurt themselves? (or indeed, starve or drug or kill themselves)', the assumption is made that there is something 'wrong' with these individuals. Their behaviour is 'maladaptive'. A psychiatric diagnosis is given, which not only explains away their feelings and behaviour as effectively their own fault, but also conveniently renders their words and actions invalid. A patient or client who believes in such an explanation and accepts that their distress and their behaviour originate in themselves (as many do), can then be helped to 'get better' without threatening anyone else's power. ('Getting better' in this context usually involves learning to cope better as an individual with the feelings and difficulties evoked by one's situation, rather than directly challenging it.)

Practitioners and their clients who do attempt to expose and challenge the status quo may soon find themselves struggling or being punished. One recent illustration of this is the promotion of the idea of 'False Memory Syndrome', which has caused many survivors of abuse and practitioners who wish to believe and support their clients to feel anxious, isolated and undermined.

The argument that mental health professionals may resist both the recognition of the role of social forces in causing distress and the empowerment of their patients does not imply that they do not genuinely care and wish to help. Rather, our argument simply reflects a view that mental health in general, and self-injury in particular, are political as well as personal issues. Self-injury is inextricably related to the social conditions within which it occurs. Professionals working with self-injury are entering a political arena where their approach implicitly reflects a political stance. Whether this stance is one which goes some way towards helping individuals cope and function better, or which goes further to support the empowerment of those oppressed by social relations is a personal choice. This choice has great implications for individual practitioners, the services within which they work, and for society as a whole.

4. The Origins and Functions of Self-Injury for Individuals

'My childhood wasn't happy. I was the eldest of five, so very soon had to take on the responsibilities of an adult, taking care of the younger ones. My parents didn't get on. There would be terrible fights. The house would be smashed up, sometimes there was blood. It was a normal thing to live with violence. We all also had a fair bit of physical abuse. I was sexually abused, which led to me trying to commit suicide. I ran away constantly.'

For most individuals self-injury seems to be associated with extremely difficult and distressing life experiences, often beginning in childhood. In this chapter we will focus on the individual who self-injures and the role played by their particular life experiences in the aetiology of their self-injury. We will identify a number of ways in which such experiences may affect the individual so that they are prone, or driven, to injure themselves. We will go on to develop our central theoretical perspective of self-injury as behaviour which originates as an adaptive response to a person's situation and which fulfils specific and complex functions.

Research into the origins of self-injury has consistently identified certain experiences as significant. Most common amongst these are abuse or maltreatment, and bereavement or loss. Research into the aetiology of self-injury has for the most part concentrated on child-hood experiences (for example, van der Kolk *et al.*, 1991). Physical and sexual abuse have been recognized for some time as childhood antecedents of self-mutilation (de Young, 1982), which in all prob-ability arises as a means of coping with the abuse. The link between childhood maltreatment and self-injury has been further underlined by studies which suggest that sizeable proportions of abused or neglected children (Green, 1978) and sexually abused adolescents (Lindberg and Distad, 1985) may go on to self-injure. Green (1978), for example, found that 41 per cent of a group of abused and neglected children engaged in headbanging, biting, burning and cutting themselves. Favazza (1993) in a review of more than 250 articles has suggested a broad link between self-mutilation and 'stressful situations' among which he includes physical or sexual abuse in childhood, or both, an early history of medical procedures or hospitalization, residence in total care institutions and parental alcoholism or depression. These situations all involve some level of maltreatment, neglect and loss of autonomy, and lead to feelings of helplessness, anger, and loss.

For people who begin to self-injure in adolescence or even in early or later childhood (the majority of those who self-injure, as was seen in *Chapter 1*), it is clear that the causes must lie in their early years. Self-injury beginning in adulthood also seems often to be related to childhood experience, but events in adult life may also be significant. Comparatively few authors up until now have examined the role of adult experiences in leading someone to self-injure. Greenspan and Samuel (1989), drawing on a very small sample, have suggested that self-injury may begin after adult experiences of rape or trauma, irrespective of childhood experiences, while Pitman (1990) and Lyons (1991) have found that adult self-injury may follow war trauma.

One of the present authors (Arnold, 1995) surveyed 76 women with a history of self-injury. A major aim of this research was to increase understanding of self-injury by investigating the partic-ipants' own interpretations of their experience. Part of the research concerned past, recent or current life experiences and circumstances which individuals felt had given rise to their own self-injury. The majority of those taking part (almost two-thirds) attributed their self-injury to childhood experiences alone. A further quarter felt that childhood and adult experiences were implicated, while only 14 per cent attributed their self-injury solely to experiences in adult life. These findings support the idea that self-injury most commonly has its roots in childhood experience, yet indicate that adult experiences and circumstances also need to be investigated in order to achieve a full understanding of the origins of an individual's self-injury.

Childhood Experiences Underlying Self-Injury

Arnold's survey found that there were several common sorts of childhood experience which participants believed had contributed to the distress which led them to self-injure. As *Table 1* shows, many women reported having suffered several of these experiences, often including multiple forms of abuse and deprivation. The two sorts of experience most frequently reported as leading individuals to self-injure were sexual abuse and neglect. Emotional abuse was also

Table 1

Childhood experiences	%[1]
Sexual abuse	49
Neglect	49
Emotional abuse	43
Lack of communication	27
Physical abuse	25
Loss/separation	25
Parent ill/alcoholic	17
Other	19

[1]Percentage of all women answering questions concerning life experiences.

reported by a large proportion of the women, while a quarter had experienced physical abuse. Some had frequently witnessed family violence, although they had not been physically abused themselves.

Significant losses in childhood included the death of parents or siblings, and prolonged or total separation from one or both parents. For a number of women, parents' illness or alcoholism led to neglect of their own needs and/or to their having to care for their parents or siblings from a young age.

'My mum was always ill. She had bad epilepsy and she also used to get terribly depressed, crying all the time. There was a lot of shame about her illnesses and we had to pretend everything was all right.'

A problem which many women reported as having exacerbated their situation as a child was lack of communication in the family. Some families allowed discussion of practical or intellectual matters, but seemed to operate a taboo about feelings or problems. This had led some women as children to attempt to communicate via their self-injury.

'Sometimes no one spoke to me for weeks. We would pass on the stairs like strangers. There were never any hugs or love, just ice-cold looks, no conversations.'

Other distress identified by some women as leading to their self-injury included being subjected to excessively high expectations within the family or school, bullying and rejection by peers, racism, and fear and shame about puberty or lesbian sexuality.

'I was under great pressure to achieve at school – I was expected to get to Oxbridge. At the same time there was all this stuff going on at home that I wasn't allowed to discuss outside the family. I just couldn't handle it all.'

The findings of this survey in respect of childhood experiences are similar to those of other sizeable studies of the backgrounds of people who self-injure. Van der Kolk *et al.* (1991) reported that in a study of 28 participants, '79% gave histories of significant childhood trauma and 89% reported major disruptions in parental care. . . . sexual abuse was most strongly related to all forms of self-destructive behaviour'. The age at which trauma occurred was significant, with the type and severity of self-destructiveness varying: the younger the child when first abused or separated from caregivers, the more cutting (as opposed to other forms of self-destructive behaviour, such as starving or binge eating, or suicide attempts), and the more severe the injuries inflicted. From follow-up studies the authors also found that self-injury was most tenacious amongst those who had the most severe histories of separation and neglect, leading them to suggest that 'although childhood trauma contributes heavily to the initiation of self-destructive behaviour, lack of secure attachments maintains it'. Walsh and Rosen (1988) found in a study of adolescents who self-injured that many had lost a parent (either through death or separation – often due to placement in care). Many of the adolescents had been physically or sexually abused, and again this factor was most strongly correlated with self-mutilation. Most seemed to come from families characterized by impulsivity, violence, alcoholism, self-destructiveness and chaos. A significant proportion had also experienced serious or chronic illness or surgery during childhood. The authors reported that many of their participants suffered further losses of various kinds in adolescence, which contributed to the 'triggering' of self-injury. These losses included the break-up of important peer relationships, relocation of family home, and separation from family due to placement in residential treatment.

Adult Experiences Underlying Self-Injury

Arnold's survey found that, where individuals related their self-injury to adult experiences, these involved similar factors to the childhood experiences reported.

As *Table 2* shows, rape and sexual abuse (or harassment) were the most frequently cited experiences. A number of women said self-injury was triggered by being emotionally or physically abused in relationships with men; others reported lack of support and communication, again usually in relationships with partners.

'As an adult my cutting got much worse after I was assaulted by my boss at work and it was all hushed up.'

Table 2

Adult experiences	%[1]
Rape/sexual abuse	22
Abusive partner	14
Lack of support/communication	13
Loss of/unable to have child	10
Other	17

[1]Percentage of all women answering questions concerning life experiences.

Other significant adult experiences mentioned included miscarriage, the loss of a child (through bereavement or separation) and inability to have children. For some women, self-injury began, or became more frequent or severe, following incarceration in prison or psychiatric hospital. Others had injured themselves to cope with the enormous feelings of loss and desperation following the break-up of a relationship. A few women reported injuring themselves following their own serious physical illness.

The Links Between Life Experiences and Self-Injury

Having established that certain childhood (and for some, adult) experiences are common in the backgrounds of people who self-injure, the question arises as to the nature of the links between such experiences and the development of this behaviour. Why should someone who has been abused or maltreated in some way, or has suffered neglect or loss, go on to repeatedly injure their own body? A number of authors have addressed this question. Walsh and Rosen (1988) suggest that childhood experiences may establish a number of 'characteristics' which make individuals prone to self-injure, namely a 'vulnerability to loss'; a 'role of victim'; a 'distorted and alienated body image'; and a 'predilection towards impulsive, self-destructive behaviour'. Others, such as van der Kolk *et al.* (1991), have suggested a biological link between childhood experiences of maltreatment and later self-injury.

In broad terms, we understand the links between traumatic experiences and self-injury in the following way. Such experiences have two major effects which may give rise to self-injury. Firstly, they force the child (or later, the adult) to experience very complex, distressing emotions in the absence of autonomous means of coping. Self-injury may then develop as the only alternative to feeling that one may not survive the experience. Secondly, such experiences, maltreatment in particular, often result in feelings of low self-worth, self-loathing, guilt and shame, which may lead someone to a tendency towards self-destructiveness. We will now further explore and develop ideas concerning a range of possible links between experiences of abuse, maltreatment, neglect or loss, and subsequent self-injury.

The legacy of distress

The sorts of life experiences and circumstances typically undergone by people who self-injure are likely to result in enormously distressing feelings. Many people who self-injure report having experienced since childhood overwhelming and unbearable feelings of sadness, grief, betrayal, anger, shame, powerlessness and anxiety. The intolerable nature of their distress leads them to a desperate search for ways of alleviating and coping with their feelings. In Arnold's survey (1995, quoted earlier) participants reported that the most frequent trigger for self-injury was overwhelming feelings of emotional pain or anger.

Abandonment and emptiness

Children who have been abused or neglected such that their needs for love and nurturance are not met, or who have suffered the loss of a primary caregiver, are likely to suffer greatly from feelings of abandonment and loss, and a terrifying sense that the world is not a safe and good place for them. Similarly, those whose caregivers made unreasonable emotional demands on them as children (and perhaps simultaneously set up excessive expectations for having their own needs met by the child) may have been left with overwhelming feelings of abandonment, rage and frustration. If such children are not supported in expressing and containing these feelings, they will not be able to learn how to manage such distress in later life. At the same time they are unable to internalize sufficient love and caring to build up their own inner resources. They are deprived of the opportunity to learn (by example) how to comfort and soothe themselves when distressed. As adults they may experience overwhelming feelings of emptiness and desperation, yet be unable to find ways of meeting their own emotional needs.

Shapiro (1987) reported that some of the women in her study of incest survivors injured themselves in response to 'unresolved fears of abandonment and separation'. Similarly, Arnold's study (1995) found that around a third of those surveyed reported that their self-injury was sometimes a means of dealing with unbearable feelings of neediness or emptiness.

Gabriel self-injured so severely that he was hospitalized on several occasions. In therapy he described his childhood upbringing as having contained many advantages and 'no problems', although he described self-mutilating since the age of ten. What emerged from his accounts of his early family life was that his parents, although fair and responsible, seemed unable to tolerate strong expressions of negative emotion in each other, or in their children. They created an environment where there were formal family discussions to deal with strong issues. There were also family rules designed to ensure consideration for all family members. Gabriel described poignantly to his therapist how he always 'forgot' the family rules, and how he could not cope with the family meetings or with his resulting feelings of rage and distress.

Powerlessness

Abuse and abandonment can cause children to experience terrifying feelings of powerlessness and helplessness, and these feelings do not necessarily abate as the child grows up. One of the ways in which previous trauma impacts on a person's capacity to cope in the here and now is in the reduction of feelings of personal effectiveness, or the sense that they can influence what happens to them. Furthermore adults who have suffered a severe childhood trauma are also thought to be more susceptible to adverse reactions to adult trauma. Traumatic situations such as domestic violence, rape, and war, are known now to have worse effects in a variety of ways (van der Kolk *et al.*, 1996) on individuals who were traumatized as children. Individuals may adopt a range of means, including self-injury, to try to overcome such feelings of powerlessness.

Difficulties in identifying, understanding and verbalizing feelings

Children need to learn from their parents or care-takers how to understand, and differentiate between, the various kinds of distress and discomfort they experience and to express these appropriately – in words, tears, and so on. Those whose environment does not allow this talk among its members, or who do not receive recognition, empathy and support for their feelings cannot learn these things. Children in abusive households may be punished for attempting to express their feelings. Opportunities for communicating and receiving support for feelings and problems may be very limited, and the child may grow up with little ability to verbalize or even identify their experiences, feelings and needs. Some individuals may have been taken good care of physically, but not emotionally. The emphasis on physical care, but the exclusion of verbal and emotional expression and resolution, may explain why later in life physical solutions to distress are the first to be reached for. A disruption in the ability to communicate emotions through words can manifest itself in individuals who find it difficult to name different emotions, or to distinguish between them, or to identify where in the body feeling responses are located. This phenomenon has been described, notably by Sifneos (1972; see also Nemiah and Sifneos, 1970), as underlying psychosomatic conditions and manifestations. Dieter and Pearlman (in press) offer this description of self-injury as a form of expression of affect: 'The individual moves from arousal to action without *mediating stages* [italics ours] of feeling awareness, feeling identification, feeling expression, and self-soothing'.

Adults who are having difficulty in making sense of what happens to them, particularly when this is distressing or harmful, will often experience difficulties in coping with feelings. Much of our capacity to deal with painful material relies on our being able to tell ourselves or others a narrative about what is happening, on processing our experience through language. People who self-injure frequently describe themselves as confused and not very good at communicating painful experiences. It would appear that individuals who are at a disadvantage with regard to verbal fluency are more at risk of being drawn to immediate *physical* 'solutions' such as self-injury.

Lily self-injured very seriously and had to be admitted to hospital on several occasions. She described having grown up in a household as the youngest of three very clever sisters. Her mother played the piano and taught music. Lily was not very good at music and did not do as well at school as her sisters. She described having been bullied by teachers who became angry at her for not concentrating in class. She felt very different because it seemed to her as though everyone around her had conversations that she did not understand, describing what they had done and talking about how they felt.

Acting out

This term has had a variety of meanings in the psychotherapeutic literature, but has often come recently to be associated in its various forms ('acting in', 're-enactment', and so on) with the area of abuse therapy. 'Acting out' tends to refer to a constellation of self-destructive or potentially dangerous acts that arise as a means of coping with abuse-specific internal conflict (Briere, 1996). What is usually referred to is that a behaviour or an act in some way *replaces* a feeling or a memory associated with a traumatic experience. This process has been seen and described by various authors in terms of how far people are along the road of integrating traumatic experiences. It is thought that re-experiencing is an earlier, pre-verbal form of expressing. Hence someone may self-injure as a means of expressing both the feelings associated with trauma, and the traumatic experience itself, as an earlier form of 'narrative', before they are ready to speak about it. The parallel may be drawn with the appropriateness to young children of acting instead of talking.

One of the more exciting and subtle functions of the body may be in recording experience which is inaccessible to conscious memory for various reasons. Bessel van der Kolk and Rita Fisler (1995) found that traumatic memories were retrieved in the form of imprints of sensory and affective elements of the traumatic experience. Events that occur in very early childhood (that is, before the development of language) cannot at first be 'remembered' through language, but are experienced as actions, whose meanings are not obvious but need to be understood gradually. Traumatic events that occur within an intimate relationship may thus be acted out alone or in intimate relationships elsewhere.

Language is crucial in the development of emotions and the formation of relationships. In some cases, language development may be slowed for various reasons. It is possible that early emotional injuries, such as neglect, in themselves impoverish the child's capacity for expressing themselves verbally. In addition, early experiences of maltreatment by care-givers are thought to impair an individual's capacity to regulate how strongly emotionally upset they become at stressful times. Thus maltreatment at the same time increases the need, but diminishes the means, of expressing painful feelings. It is not difficult to understand how in such circumstances self-mutilation will present itself as a means of expression.

The reality of the bad parent

A child who has been maltreated by their parent needs very strongly to continue to believe in that parent nevertheless. Part of this phenomenon is the desire on the part of the child to remove from their awareness 'bad' parts of their parents' personalities and bad moments in their relationships with their parents. This enables the creation of a new 'ideal' parent, who is free of horrible attributes (Bollas, 1995).

Children who have not been maltreated do this with their parents. It is thought to be a normal developmental process, whereby a child comes to grips with the realization that they themselves as well as their parents are a mixture of 'good' and 'bad' aspects. Bollas (1995) has proposed that what maltreatment does, is to make it impossible for this process to happen normally. Because the parent was *in reality* bad, abusive, out of control, or monstrous, it is impossible for the developing child to safely 'play with' ideas of them as good and bad. Furthermore, because the parent violated the child's trust in reality, they are always, and tragically, tarnished. This means that the child's capacity for also seeing themselves as a mixture of good and bad is diminished, and with it their ability to find their 'good' self, and to experience themselves (and their parent) comfortably. In later life, the adult, perhaps after a period of experiencing themselves as 'bad' cannot find comfort, but needs something external to themselves, such as self-injury, to help them make the transition back to a 'good' and coping self.

Living with the abuser

It may also be the case that any affection, attention and physical contact or pleasure a child received in their family was associated with abuse. Periods of calm or affection between passages of violence and neglect may satisfy a child's wish to be in the wonderful care of the parent, relaxed, contained, safe and connected. Bollas (1995) has elaborated this idea, discussing how the renewal (reparation) of the parent each time comes to signify that the terror has ended, the abandonment is not permanent, and the 'good parent' is once again available. In this situation, the abusive parent (or later another significant person) is the only parent (other) available, and the passages of good caring have to be reached as the after-effects of maltreatment. The internalization of this process may set up a similar relationship to the self, which is then re-enacted in self-mutilation. Self-injury or physical damage is something which has to be gone through in order to be able to care for the self, to gratify feelings of being vulnerable and needing protection and comfort.

One woman who injured herself by means of severe cutting and burning described how, following a childhood characterized by violence, deprivation and sexual abuse, she married a man who treated her abusively:

'My marriage failed because of my husband's violence and his confirmation that I was no good: the way I dressed, the way I looked. I was being raped and abused in horrific and humiliating ways but could say nothing to anyone. I was totally alone, too afraid to have a friend or a conversation. The only way I found of coping was to self-harm.'

In adult life this process may wrongly be seen by others as an 'addiction', both in the case of self-injury and in other situations where a person appears to be a participant in violence towards the self (for example, when women appear unable to desist from returning to live with a violent partner). In fact, the victim of battering (or of self-mutilation) may be unwilling to accept the violence, but have no other means of experiencing the pleasurable nurturing which relief (in the form of an apologetic, tender partner or the cessation of self-injury) brings.

Self-loathing

The sorts of abusive experiences which many people who self-injure have undergone often lead to a range of extremely negative feelings about the self, including shame, self-blame and guilt, low self-esteem, self-hatred and the conviction that one is 'bad', 'evil', or 'dirty'. This may be partly as a result of direct teaching, usually by the abuser, which may include denigrating remarks and the assertion that the reason for what is happening to the child is their own ugliness, badness, and worthlessness. It may also be the child's way of attempting to understand their experience and to hold on to the belief that their parents are 'good', and would love them, if only they themselves were sufficiently good and loveable. Clearly negative feelings induced about the self do not always lead people to self-injure, but they seem to be an important pre-condition for self-injury amongst those who do choose this way of dealing with their experiences and feelings.

One woman described such feelings vividly:

'I disgust myself so much I need punishing. Cutting is the only way I know how. I hate myself so much for who I am and what I have become. Fat, ugly, vile, bitter, disgusting and dirty. I don't want anyone to touch me, I am so revolting . . . Thinking of myself as ugly and disgusting is now true and evident to others – they only have to see my arms.'

Wise (1990) sees shame as central to self-injury, arguing that children who are abused internalize the shame and victimization which may have characterized their families for generations, developing 'shame-based survival skills' (including self-mutilation) to cope with their experiences. Bonnie Burstow (1992) understands the self-hatred described by many women who self-injure as an expression of 'internalised oppression' – the process by which the individual takes into herself the hatred and denigration she has received from others, believing she is to blame for their views and treatment of her.

The relationship to the body

A frequent consequence of traumatic and painful childhood experiences which has relevance for self-injury is alienation from, and hatred of, one's own body. (This is separate from, yet clearly related to hatred of the self.) Walsh and Rosen (1988) report that children who are seriously and chronically ill are often confused about their bodies, seeing them as ugly, disfigured and unacceptable. They may perceive their bodies as unintegrated with and separate from themselves. Body alienation has similarly been noted amongst children who have been sexually and/or physically abused. Sgroi (1982) reported that children who had been sexually abused viewed their bodies as contaminated and dirty, as well as alien and 'traitorous' to themselves.

Self-mutilation is an attack on the **body** first and foremost, and clearly the feelings and perceptions the individual has about their body are highly significant in respect of self-injury. Someone who loathes and rejects their own body, perhaps blaming it for being vulnerable, sick, hurt or abused, and seeing it as alien or 'other', is far more likely to feel willing, or even compelled, to injure and 'punish' that body, or misuse it or treat it disrespectfully.

The significance of the skin

The most common forms of self-injury involve mutilation of the skin (as well as possibly, deep tissue) – cutting, scraping, picking, burning, and so on. In fact, in our experience, for many people, self-injury which does **not** involve breaking the skin (for example, banging and bruising) is not experienced as so effective or 'satisfying'. It seems likely, therefore, that factors concerning the skin itself may be significant in self-injury.

Dinora Pines (1980; 1993) describes some important psychological functions of the skin. Between infants and their mothers the skin acts as a means of communication and contact, through which comfort is given (through holding) and the pleasures of touch, warmth, taste and smell are experienced. The skin is also the container of self, representing the boundary between self and non-self. Mothers (and other care-givers) may communicate a whole range of emotions to the child through their handling of their body, their skin (as felt by the child's skin) conveying love and warmth, or disgust and hate. A neglected child who is not held, comforted and kept clean will also experience this in part through their skin, which is not touched, held and soothed as the child needs, but may in fact feel cold, wet and sore. Pines describes how a child's distress may find expression through the skin in disorders such as eczema – 'The skin may itch, the skin may weep, and the skin may rage' (Pines, 1980, p.315) .

Abuse of children frequently involves the skin, which is broken and wounded or through which pain is experienced. Some forms of abuse (such as rape) may also involve a breach of the child's physical and self-boundaries, which are delineated by the skin.

The great psychological significance of the skin and the involvement of the skin in the experiences of abuse, abandonment, neglect and rejection point to an important link with self-mutilation. Skin sensations re-establish self-boundaries, both symbolically and through immediate physical experience. Further, because acts of self-injury are often followed by taking care of the skin, this may provide soothing for which an individual longs. Skin mutilation also re-creates boundary violations, which an individual may re-enact in an attempt to understand or resolve their experience.

Melody was adopted as an infant, following her teenage mother giving her up and a series of foster placements. Her adoptive mother told her that when she first got her home she would lie for hours unresponsively and that this was because her natural mother and foster carers hardly ever picked her up and held her. Melody's adoptive parents placed a lot of importance on good behaviour, table manners and cleanliness, and sent her to dance lessons and various sports activities. However, both were physically abusive and extremely emotionally distant. Melody cut herself throughout her teens and early twenties, as a means of coping with the floods of anger and loneliness which overcame her every time she thought about her childhood. In the early stages of therapy she ceased to cut herself, but an existing skin condition which she had suffered since childhood worsened drastically and erupted at times of stress and perceived abandonment by her therapist.

Difficulties with relationships

People who have been abused, neglected or abandoned as children may experience difficulties in forming supportive, intimate relationships. Walsh and Rosen's (1988) study of teenagers who self-injured found many to have particular difficulties in sustaining supportive relationships with peers, which were instead often 'short-term, conflictual and combative'. Deprived of supportive relationships as children, individuals may find it very hard to trust and open themselves to others, or to seek appropriate support and empathy from others when they are feeling needy or distressed. They may also find themselves in relationships which replicate the difficult mixture of excessive expectation and disappointment which characterized their childhood relationships. This means that they are more likely to feel forced to play out their conflicts and feelings in isolation rather than in relationship to others, sometimes in ways involving injury to their own bodies.

Difficulties with separation/individuation

Abuse, neglect, loss and abandonment may all interfere with the important tasks of psychological separation from parents and the development of an individuated self. In an abusive family the child's existential (as well as physical) boundaries may be repeatedly violated. She may be isolated from others outside the family and forced to maintain a high degree of identification and loyalty with those who abuse her. She may be consistently expected to anticipate and respond to her parents' needs and feelings, suppressing her own or seeing these as synonymous with theirs. Even a child who is not actually abused but who does not receive sufficient nurturance (or who loses this prematurely) may have no secure foundation from which to dare to become a separate person. The resulting lack of differentiation and confusion between oneself and one's parents (and later, others) may continue into adulthood.

This may relate to self-injury in a number of ways. On the one hand, self-mutilation may be an attempt to identify and assert one's own physical and self-boundaries. It is as if the person were saying 'This is me. Here is where I begin and end.' On the other hand the person may be so closely identified (or confluent) with another person that they may feel that they can express their anger or desire to punish them on their own bodies. This applies particularly to individuals who were subjected to rape at a very young age or in such a manner as to set up actual confusion about whose body is whose, and who is doing what to whom. Self-injury on the part of someone who has been abused may also be a means of continuing the abuse on behalf of the parent. The individual's loyalty to their parents (or their terror of and inability to distinguish themselves from them and thus 'lose' what little they have of them) may drive them to hurt themselves as a way of effectively saying, 'You are good, what you did to me was right'.

Violence and abuse are normal modes of relating/behaving

Many people who self-injure come from families where violence and impulsive or chaotic behaviour are routine. It is not unreasonable to suppose that observation of these ways of relating and dealing with life may contribute in part to some individuals' propensity to injure themselves in response to their own distress or difficulties.

Melody became known to the therapy services as a result of her many emotional and physical problems. She had been imprisoned for violent crimes from an early age. She had been treated for addictions. She self-injured for many years and suffered from outbreaks of very severe physical symptoms including chronic pain and psoriasis. Melody described growing up in a household in which severe beatings and emotional abuse were common. Her parents were very 'respectable' and episodes of extreme violence towards the children were construed as deserved punishment. Melody described these violent episodes as the parents 'going mad'. Episodes of beating with objects, screaming verbal abuse and shouting encouragement to each other alternated with rigidly controlled behaviour where the parents emphasized 'manners'.

Fossum and Mason (1986) suggest a process in many families in which abuse takes place whereby there is an 'oscillation between compulsive control and abusive release'. The 'release' or 'breakout phase' involves a range of destructive and abusive behaviours (which allow the individual to escape the pressures of control and shame), involving alcohol, drugs, food, sex, money, self-mutilation and abuse of others. Wise (1990) suggests that children growing up in such families are taught 'a self-abusive pattern of surviving stress, pain, injury and betrayal'.

Dissociation

Many children and adults cope with traumatic experiences by numbing themselves, both physically and emotionally, or by distancing themselves from present awareness of themselves and their environment. This kind of dissociation may recur in later life even in the absence of external threat. Some people report 'finding themselves' injuring during a dissociated state. Others find that the sensation and shock of an injury to themselves can help them to regain feelings of being alive, real and present.

Possible biological links

Some researchers have concentrated exclusively on the biological aspects of self-injury, identifying various possible elements involved in the processes as giving rise to the behaviour. Van der Kolk *et al.* (1991) have suggested a biological link between childhood experiences and self-injury. They propose that a degree of biological predisposition to self-injure can arise from the experience of maltreatment in early childhood. Anatomical pathways set up in response to extreme stress during childhood may 'program' the individual such that they perform biologically in a similar fashion during subsequent stressful experiences.

Endorphins (naturally occurring opiates in the brain) are thought to be implicated in the regulation of emotional states. It has been proposed that the opiate system of some individuals has been impaired such that they need external means to stimulate the release of additional opiates. These opiates bring about analgesia, reducing anxiety and maintaining a psychological and biological balance. The pain and physical trauma from self-mutilation are thought to stimulate the release of endorphins that maintain this balance. Winchel and Stanley (1991) reviewed the research pertaining to this theory, but the exact relationship between opiate release and self-mutilation seems unclear, however. It is possible, some authors argue (Haines *et al.*, 1995) that the extreme stress that *precedes* an episode of self-mutilation is what causes the analgesia, and not the injury itself.

The serotonergic system has also been associated with self-injury (see, for example, Winchel and Stanley, 1991; Simeon *et al.*, 1992). This body of work does seem to suggest that self-injury is a disorder of impulse control, caused by impaired serotonin levels. At the moment however, the speculation concerning the role of serotonin in self-destructive behaviours awaits full empirical validation.

The Importance of the Physical Aspects of Self-Injury

Whilst we are not convinced by evidence of a biological explanation for self-injury, it is clear to us that the physical aspects of self-injury are extremely important. Pain, bleeding and scarring can contribute to the effectiveness of self-injury (as a means of dealing with their experience) for the individual.

From our experience, different individuals have different experiences of pain when injuring themselves. Some appear to feel little or no pain at the time of injuring, although wounds often cause considerable pain later:

'I don't feel any pain when I cut myself. To me the deeper the cut is the better.'

'Usually I don't feel any pain, but I think I feel it now more than I used to, maybe that's because I'm learning to be scared of injuring myself.'

For others, feeling pain at the time is very important:

'Pain is part of the punishment, but it doesn't last long enough.'

'Sometimes I burn myself rather than cutting because that hurts more. I suppose in a way it takes your mind off what you feel inside. But in a way it also kind of proves you're human, and how much you're hurting.'

For many people, bleeding seems important in providing some of the functions of self-injury:

'I liked the bleeding. It was like tears, but I didn't have to cry. My mother used to laugh at me if I cried.'

'When I see the blood, it's such a relief, it's like all the awfulness is coming out, and I know I'll be all right now.'

Often, people are not 'satisfied' with an injury unless it leaves a mark or scar:

'I have to do it so it shows, a decent scar. Then I know it's real, it matters.'

It is unlikely that a single simple theory, biological or otherwise, could account for a behaviour as complex as self-mutilation. Any framework for understanding this behaviour has to include emotional, cognitive, inter-personal and intrapsychic processes. What comes through to us from our work with individuals is that the physical aspects of self-injury are central to the psychological motivations and functions of the behaviour. The biological angle is entirely consistent with powerful psychological explanations, such as those presented by John Briere's (1996) theories of tension-reduction and the learning of extremely avoidant means of coping with distress arising from abuse in childhood. The tension-reduction model (see also Favazza, 1989) with its physical and psychological aspects fits with the phenomenology of self-mutilation. The links between psychological and biological explanations need to be explored further, as van der Kolk and his colleagues continue to do in relation to childhood abuse. Other directions for this type of research may implicate environmental conditions such as imprisonment and solitary confinement. The full complexity of psycho-physiological changes in self-mutilation remains to be understood, in our view, and simple models of the relationship between physical and psychological aspects seem unlikely to contribute to this understanding.

The Functions of Self-Injury for the Individual

In our exploration of the nature of the links between life experiences and self-injury we have mentioned various purposes which injuring oneself may serve. In this section we will explore further the many powerful and complex ways in which self-injury may function in the lives and relationships of people who have been subjected to such experiences.

1. *Functions concerned with coping and surviving*

For many people, self-injury serves as a means of coping and carrying on with life in spite of enormous psychological distress. To cut or hurt oneself may be felt to be life-saving, rather than self-destructive:

'Burning myself with caustic soda has a survival purpose for me. It stops me killing myself and enables me to cope with the pain and torment I sometimes feel.'

'After I've cut, things never seem so bad. I sometimes wonder if I'll ever give up, because it feels safe to be doing this. It sounds silly, I know, but it's like knowing the exact way to handle a situation.'

There are a number of particular ways in which self-injury seems to help individuals to cope with unbearable feelings:

The regulation of distress and anxiety

One of the most commonly reported functions of self-mutilation is the regulation of distress and anxiety. When feelings become intolerable, self-injury can serve a self-soothing or tension-reducing function:

'When I cut myself it takes away all the self-hate and all the feelings I have inside. It's like a self-release.'

'The more deliberate it is, the more instant is the relief. It's like piercing a bloated sac, letting air and light in and oozy liquid out.'

We have seen that self-injury is particularly prevalent in the prison population. The following account describes the experience of one prison inmate who cut himself every few days:

'The things that make me cut are feeling like you're going out of your head and like you're a time-bomb waiting to go off, and knowing that if you cut you will feel better.'

For some people the role of bleeding is central in reducing distress and tension:

'My pain had reached fever-pitch, almost to explosion point, and to let it out I had to cut myself. When I saw the blood flowing I felt it was coming out at last.'

'I resist cutting myself until I am desperate to get rid of the anger, self-disgust, contempt and pain, that go on and on until I need the blood to flow. The feeling of watching all that go down the sink makes me elated.'

It is interesting that this function can apply even without actual self-injury taking place there and then; the fact that the individual knows that she has this means of relieving her feelings at her disposal can help her to get through periods of intense anxiety, perhaps by reducing her sense of helplessness in the face of her distress:

'Self-harm has become like a friend to me. When things go wrong and I am badly hurting I know I can turn to self-harm. I keep a bag of broken glass

by my bed. Sometimes I go to sleep holding a piece of broken glass that I may or may not later use. It gives me a sense of security.'

It is notable how frequently people who self-injure say that this seems an entirely reasonable or inevitable means of coping with their feelings:

'After my child was born I was very depressed; cutting seemed inevitable, logical, sensible, and the only thing to do to cope with terrible feelings.'

'When I have feelings of anxiety or panic, it feels like a logical conclusion. This has just got to happen.'

What comes across is the relative manageability and the benign nature of self-mutilation in comparison to the enormity of the distress and tension experienced. This point is helpful for workers who are trying to understand someone who does not appear to be as distressed about their self-injury as they themselves are.

Dealing with anger

'The reason I self-harm is that I am angry about everything – the past, being put in prison, the treatment I have had from psychiatry and the threats of going to Broadmoor.'

It seems to be difficult in our society to express anger acceptably. This may be because anger carries with it connotations of violence and loss of control. Theoretically, it should be possible to express one's anger, to be heard and for no one to get hurt, but the reality is that for most people the experience of anger is an altogether more dangerous one. This is particularly the case for women, who feel more unsafe both in expressing and receiving anger.

If it is difficult to express anger directly, people will look for other means which carry the same powerful emotions. Many people who self-injure say that this is a means by which they deal with what feels like intolerable anger:

'Sometimes when I am angry to the point of physical harm an image of the act comes to me. I remember being so angry once while I was pushing food down a waste-disposal unit that I felt like I wanted to shove my arm down there with all the garbage. It wasn't the pain of the experience I was anticipating, so much as the violence and brute force of it.'

Many people are hard on themselves and turn their anger onto what they perceive to be their inadequacies or shortcomings. For people who self-injure, hurting themselves can serve as both a punishment for these 'shortcomings' and a manifestation of this intense anger at the self:

'I used to get very angry with myself, so I hurt myself as a punishment for being so awful – fat, ugly, thick, no friends, parents hated me, never have a boyfriend, etc. etc.'

Often when people direct their anger at themselves, it seems as though they are perceiving their bodies as something separate and not part of the self:

'I got very angry that no one would listen to me and accept that there was anything wrong with me, and this made me hurt myself by swallowing stuff.'

Sometimes individuals self-injure as a way of releasing anger without hurting others. Whether they would actually hurt someone else does not seem relevant – the fantasy that one might is sufficient:

'I cut myself instead of having a go at others. The moment I see the blood coming from my cuts I feel so relaxed, and not frustrated and angry any more.'

Distraction: focusing the pain to make it manageable

A second major way in which self-injury seems to help people cope with unbearable feelings is avoidance. The injury takes the person's attention away from their distress and anxiety and onto something which feels more manageable:

'It helps to take some of the pain away. When I want to run and can't, then I cut. When I wish I had a good father, I want to cut. When I have memories that I don't want to deal with, then I want to cut.'

'I feel so much emotional pain that I have to turn it into a physical pain which is easier to accept and understand; it distracts me from my feelings.'

Physical pain may be important in allowing the person to escape for a while from their emotional agony:

'I would leave cuts in the hope they wouldn't heal too soon, the pain seems to drain away the agony leading up to such situations – the longer the pain goes on, the longer the bad feelings are postponed.'

What is notable about self-injury is its ability to serve a useful distraction or avoidance function without substantially altering awareness, unlike, for example, substance abuse. Coping methods such as alcohol, drugs, or over-sleeping, may have far more pervasive effects on an individual's life and work. This may explain why some people who appear to be saying, 'I can't face this right now' may self-injure rather than, for example, drinking, so that they are then able to go back to work or get on with their lives and responsibilities:

'It was a way of coping while blocking out the demands which the world put on me.'

2.   Functions concerning the self

Increasing one's sense of autonomy and control

For many people, self-injury provides a sense of having control over something, of exercising autonomy and being in charge of one's own life. Often people in situations such as prisons or severely abusive families are reduced to self-injury as their sole means of deriving any sense of agency or feeling that they have the power to make things happen. Simpson (1977) suggested that the act of self-mutilation allows the individual 'to be aggressor and aggressed, actor and acted upon, punisher and punished':

'When I hurt those parts of my body I felt more in control afterwards, like I was in charge of my body and it wasn't in charge of me.'

The pain of self-injury may be an important part of the process of feeling in control, and perhaps proud of one's autonomy and strength:

'Even when it really hurts I make myself do it, so I feel I can do it. It makes me feel in control.'

Sometimes there is a sense that self-injury enables the person to reclaim something of themselves:

*'I scar myself as a sign that it's **my** body.'*

Related to this function of exerting autonomy and control, is a sense of a boundary being crossed, a risk taken, or a taboo broken. It is as though the individual needs to state (to themselves if not to anyone else) that they need not bow to every restriction, nor be limited by what is allowed by others:

'Every time I did it, I knew I was doing something wrong.'

'Another aspect of it, which may sound really sick, is the excitement involved in the actual cutting. How brave can I be? How much blood? How many cuts? How deep, how fatal?'

Feeling reality

Sometimes people do not feel as though they are fully in the moment, actually living through their experiences. This phenomenon, which in its extremes is referred to as dissociation or depersonalization, may be experienced as feeling numb in the body, being not quite 'there', losing time, or feeling dead or as though one is in a dream. This may originate as a protective function, but itself can be very distressing and frightening. Self-mutilation can shock the system into a sharp return to reality and end these episodes of absence from full experience:

'It's like pinching myself awake.'

'I self-harm in order to feel real when I feel dead.'

Although many people are sufficiently present in their experience to know that they want to end the feeling of being cut off, and choose to self-injure to do so, others begin to self-mutilate whilst still in a dissociated state:

'Sometimes the first thing I know is I'm just doing it.'

'I wake up and there's blood on me and I don't remember.'

An opportunity for self-nurture

'After cutting myself I go into "nurse-mode" and can enjoy taking care of my wounds.'

The period following self-injury may, for some people, provide their only opportunity to experience physical caring and comfort. Whether or not there is physical pain, the person feels they have been through something and so now 'deserve' some special caring:

'I think the result of hurting myself is so that I can "see" the mental pain and at last I can feel sorry for myself, otherwise it wouldn't be acknowledged, and I'd carry on as "normal" until I was in a right state.'

'When I take care of my burns it's like a reason to love myself, as though I'm saying "there, there" to myself.'

3. Functions concerned with dealing with one's experience

Demonstration or expression to oneself of one's experience

For many people who self-injure, horrible and traumatic past experiences have been denied, minimized or ignored. An individual may feel self-injury to be a form of testimony: a way of being true to themselves and honouring their own experience and resulting feelings:

'I wanted to cut so I could see the pain that was within me. There was eventually a result to the years of torment I was put through. THIS IS WHAT THEY HAVE DONE TO ME.'

'I have been miserable almost from the day I was born, and I had no idea that there was any other way of feeling. I didn't have the opportunity to talk about the way I was feeling, but something in me needed to register the distress, kind-of like a prisoner tapping on the pipes.'

Injuries may provide evidence of courage and endurance as well as of suffering. This may explain why people who self-injure can feel proud (as well as ashamed) of their wounds and scars (a fact which workers may find difficult to accept):

'Even though no one else sees it, it is something I can look at. Somehow it makes the pain I feel inside real and important.'

'I was very proud of my scars, they were like battle-scars – proof of what I had been through.'

Re-enactment

Sometimes, however, what comes through from an individual is that self-mutilation is providing a replication of the circumstances of an abusive situation: the emotions, the fear, and strangely enough the 'comfort' (or at least familiarity) associated with the experience:

'I was used to physical torture all my life, and without it I felt scared and alone, and so I would recreate the abuse myself.'

'When I'm feeling really empty and frightened I'll sometimes hurt myself. It seems like the only thing to do. It's horrible, but it also comforts me somehow.'

The re-enactment function of self-injury has received a lot of attention from writers recently (Miller, 1994). What can unfortunately follow from this view of self-injury is a 'How can you do this to yourself?' attitude:

'My psychiatrist said to me, "What you're doing to yourself is as bad as what your father did to you". I can't explain why, but it made me feel very ashamed.'

For individuals who have been maltreated (especially sexually abused) in childhood the processes of emotional and physiological arousal may have become confused and overwhelming. In adulthood they may be unable to distinguish effectively between different forms of arousal, such as fear, rage, emotional need, sexual arousal or the intense experience of cutting:

'When I get turned on watching films, I want to cut myself. It's exactly the same feeling.'

In our opinion, although it can be interesting to make the connection between 'what was done to me' and 'what I'm doing to myself', this is a somewhat marginal strategy for understanding self-injury.

4. Functions concerned with self-punishment and sacrifice

Self-punishment

Some people who as children were made to feel bad, contaminated, or evil, self-injure as a means of responding to these feelings. The self-mutilation may operate as a punishment or atonement. In that painful situation someone will feel as though she deserves the injury, pain, and the tangible evidence of her shame, because she is so bad and worthless. It is almost as if there is a 'punishing self' who delivers the injury and at the same time a 'guilty self' who deserves it. Following the 'punishment' the person can forgive herself and feel absolved and relieved of some of her supposed guilt and badness for a while.

'I hurt myself as a punishment for being selfish or not trying hard enough.'

'After I do a burn or cut I can forgive myself and feel a bit sorry for myself, instead of feeling like I'm the worst person in the world.'

This is a particularly complex set of phenomena. In our experience, the self-destructive aspects of self-injury do not simply constitute the straightforward relationship 'I've done it, so I feel better' just described. Sometimes self-injury seems to act as a testament to (rather than as a relief from) someone's self-loathing:

'I get frustrated because I can never make myself as ugly as I really am.'

'I feel guilty if I don't cut, that I don't hate myself enough.'

Scarring can have complex functions in this respect, sometimes carrying both a self-enhancing element, yet also reinforcing self-hatred:

'The scars are a kind of proof that I exist, but they are also a reminder of how much I need to injure myself.'

'I have to be careful to keep my dressing gown on when I'm feeling this way, and make sure I don't see my cuts, otherwise I feel so ashamed I have to cut all over again.'

The powerful self-hating and punishing aspect of self-injury may not be as amenable to the substitution of alternatives to self-mutilation as are some of the other functions discussed. The person's underlying conviction that they are bad, wrong and dirty will need to change before the need for self-injury will recede, and this may take considerable time and work.

Cleansing and excising

A related function is that of 'cleansing' or purging. Some people feel they rid themselves of 'dirt', 'badness' or 'contamination' (and of the associated painful feelings) for a while by hurting themselves:

'I felt I was bleeding the bad bits out.'

'Having cut myself I felt cleansed and pure.'

Less commonly, an individual may feel that by injuring herself she is ridding herself of some aspect of the abuser she feels has been left inside herself.

Extreme mutilation such as internal cutting of the genitals is one of the most upsetting forms of self-injury. For the individual it can be a dramatic means of dealing with childhood abuse and the extreme emotions engendered by this:

'I self-harmed to take away the emotional pain and to try and cut out my father, his friends and the men that gang-raped me. I have used a knife and broken bottles to cut out my father from within.'

Punishing the abuser

This function is complex, and not immediately accessible to understanding. We have talked with some individuals who, in moments of extreme anger at what has been done to them, lash out at an abuser by punishing their own bodies. It is as though the body becomes totally unimportant in its own right, and is purely representative of the person that deserves the punishment:

'When I cut myself I feel as though I'm doing it to him, the bastard.'

Dealing with confusion about sexual feelings

Fear and shame about sexual arousal may also lead directly to self-mutilation. The physiological experience of sexual arousal may be confusing and dangerous for someone with a history of violent sexual trauma. It may have become associated with intolerable distress or longing and intense emotional pain. The effect of self-injury can be to deal with these feelings in an immediate physical way, which is seen as preferable to sexual release:

'I often cut myself in an attempt to rid my body of sexual feelings. It's one way of getting rid of the dirt'.

'I scald myself to stop myself being sexual.'

Where, in the aftermath of maltreatment, individuals find that arousal or masturbation are associated with fantasies of violence or sexual abuse, the disgust and self-loathing which may follow can lead to self-mutilation as a form of punishment or atonement:

'If I hear or even think of something ghastly, I just have to do it [masturbate] and then I think what kind of person am I, and that's when I hurt my hands.'

5.   Functions concerning relationships with others

Whilst, in our experience, self-injury most commonly serves internal functions for the individual, sometimes it seems that people hurt themselves in order to have some impact on others in their lives.

Communication

Self-injury may serve for some people as an attempt at communication with others. The individual feels unable to voice directly what they wish to communicate, or believes (perhaps rightly) that if they do speak this will have little effect. Self-injury often seems to be a means of trying to send out a signal that something is wrong, in the hope that someone will indicate willingness to hear more:

'I wanted someone to ask me why I was doing it. Then I would have been able to talk about my past.'

A person may feel that speech is simply not powerful enough to convey their distress or have it recognized by others:

'The drawing of blood is a way of saying "Look how bad it is, do you believe me now?"'

'I always had to do drastic things to get my mum's attention, and so I carried this on into adulthood. I don't think people will believe me if I just tell them how I feel, so I do this to show them.'

Interestingly, whilst some people injure themselves in the hope of receiving a sympathetic response, others seem to do so in order to communicate the 'badness' they feel to be inside themselves. Perhaps they wish to repel others. Alternatively they may want to show what they feel to be their 'real' but unacceptable (for example, angry, hateful, out of control, not coping) selves. At some level they may hope that others will, after all accept them as they are. Or they may hope that in so doing they may be able to shed unrealistic expectations:

'I feel bad inside, but people think I'm nice.'

'It lets me demonstrate to myself and to others how much I hate myself, and that I'm really not okay.'

Punishing others

Workers, family members and friends of people who self-injure often feel 'punished' by the behaviour. Often this is not the direct intention of the person injuring themselves, who is more concerned with regulating their own feelings. However, it does seem that sometimes self-injury is carried out with the intention of upsetting others with whom the individual feels angry. The message being given may be 'It's your fault', or 'You've let me down':

'I've never said anything to my father about what he did to me. But he hates my scars. It's like they're a reproach to him – he can't pretend nothing has happened, or that it hasn't hurt me.'

Self-mutilation can be a very angry gesture in sexual relationships. Presenting a 'spoiled' body gives the sexual partner a message which may be intended to upset or punish:

'I had cut myself and I knew I could talk my girlfriend into sleeping with me one last time because she felt so guilty. When I took my clothes off and she saw the scars I felt bad at how upset she looked.'

Influencing others' behaviour

Self-injury may be a means of trying to influence one's situation, or others' behaviour. It may constitute an attempt to get others to provide what one does not feel able to obtain directly. Perhaps the individual hopes it may influence others to be nice to them or to do things for them. Often people who find it difficult to ask for help or caring use self-injury as a means of obtaining some nurture:

'I self-harmed because I was afraid I was going to be sent home from hospital. I wanted to stay there, where I felt safe, but I couldn't say why I was scared to go home.'

'Cutting let me go to the nurse with an excuse to be cared for.'

This function is often recognized by others who feel angry at what they feel to be 'manipulation'. What needs to be understood is that self-injury here is the resort of someone who has been made to feel powerless. Even when they are in a situation where others will listen and take seriously their feelings and wants, it may take a long time for them to learn to risk asking more directly for what they need.

Self-injury may be a way of pushing others away, of trying to keep oneself safe, and perhaps discourage abuse:

'I needed to keep them away from me. I believed that if they could see how much pain I was in and that I was hurting myself then they wouldn't hurt me any more.'

A direct attempt may be made via self-injury to protect the body from unwanted sexual attention or molestation by making it 'ugly' or 'dangerous':

'I wonder if I'd done this when I was little, maybe my vagina would have stayed safe like children's are supposed to. It brings a sense of calm and rightness for a while. It would be better to keep blades in there all the time, maybe to keep me safe always.'

Summary

In this chapter we have seen that the difficult childhood (and in some cases adult) experiences typically suffered by individuals who self-injure can affect the individual in profound and far-reaching ways. Experiences of abuse, trauma, loss, deprivation and abandonment interfere with the development of a secure sense of self and a comfortable view of oneself and one's body. They inhibit language development and the ability to deal with and communicate one's experiences and feelings. Relationships with and perceptions of others may be greatly distorted. Such experiences overwhelm the child (or adult), yet interfere with or undermine her capacity to cope with them. At the same time the person may be taught modes of behaving and dealing with their experiences and feelings which emphasize physical solutions or destructiveness and so foster the development of self-injury.

For people affected in such ways, self-injury may serve an array of powerful functions. Hurting themselves may feel central to their ability to cope and carry on with life, to deal with the pain, self-hatred and confusion they feel.

The fact that self-injury is highly functional, and that it serves a variety of complex purposes at the same time for any individual, means that it is not going to be easily and simply overcome. It is not surprising that self-injury often continues for so long, or that for many individuals it is so difficult to replace with other means of coping, despite considerable work and determination.

Chapter 7 will illustrate how attempts to provide effective therapeutic help to people who harm themselves can reflect a full understanding of the profound and complex nature of the individual experiences and processes underlying the problem of self-injury.

5. Principles in Working with People who Self-Injure

We have become very aware in our training and professional contacts of the anxiety and uncertainty which self-injury seems to raise. Some agencies and individual practitioners are unwilling (or feel unable) to work at all with people who self-injure, with the result that it can be very difficult for individuals to access help or for agencies to make appropriate referrals. We have met many workers who feel dissatisfied with the kinds of responses which are frequently offered to self-injury, but who are unsure what else to do to 'get it right'. Indeed, this has been a major impetus for us in writing this book.

Those working in settings as diverse as hospitals, general practice surgeries, community mental health services, social services, prisons, children's homes, counselling services, helplines, drug and alcohol projects, supported housing and many others are likely to encounter people who injure themselves. Yet most professional training gives scant attention to the issue of self-injury. There is often little guidance or information available for those wishing to help someone who self-injures, and there may be considerable disagreement within and between agencies about the approaches which should be taken to people who self-injure. Working with people who injure themselves also inevitably raises many difficult issues and feelings for professionals, but there is often little support for those struggling with these.

In this chapter we set out some principles which we believe to be helpful in working with people who injure themselves. Although these are of necessity quite broad, we believe that readers working in any setting will find useful ideas here which can be applied in ways appropriate to their own roles and work contexts. (In *Chapter 6* we will go on to consider some practice issues and guidelines for particular settings in which self-injury may be encountered.) The chapter concludes with a discussion of training and support for staff.

General Principles for Effective Working

Awareness of self-injury

The first requirement for effective working is that staff are aware of, and alert to, self-injury. Many people who injure themselves are ashamed, afraid and secretive, and they may not raise the subject unless they feel the worker knows about it and will not condemn them. On the other hand, they are often desperate to talk about (and perhaps gain help with) the problem, and the distress which under-lies it. It is important for self-injury to be picked up as early as possi-ble, so that it does not become entrenched, and serious underlying problems missed.

'The first GP I told about it was awful. He hadn't got a clue. Then he just took me off his list when I was in a crisis. The GP I go to now is much more understanding, and treats me with dignity and respect.'

Willingness to hear about self-injury will often communicate itself naturally, but workers may wish to help people to raise the topic, where appropriate. This can be done non-intrusively by making it clear through literature or general information/conversation that self-injury is something which an agency (or individual worker) is familiar with. In some cases a worker may feel it appropriate to respond to hints or signs of self-injury. An individual may have vis-ible wounds, bruises or recent scars, or dressings may be evident. A gentle, tactful enquiry along the lines of 'Have you hurt yourself?' (rather than a demand for explanation) may encourage the person to reveal that they are injuring themselves. Alternatively, individuals may give verbal clues by talking in terms of 'not feeling safe', 'being worried what they might do' and so on, which staff can invite them to elaborate on. Workers may fear being intrusive or upsetting some-one by encouraging them to raise the topic of self-injury, but in our experience, many individuals are very relieved to be helped to talk about the issue. If questions are framed as invitations which can be taken up or not, rather than as interrogation, intrusiveness can be avoided.

'I used to sit in college with my sleeve sort-of accidentally half pushed up, hoping someone would see the marks and ask me what was wrong.'

It is useful for agencies to have some information available for clients (and possibly for their families if appropriate) about self-injury and about sources of help and support. Until recently, it has been very difficult for people who self-injure to find any accessible literature or other material to help them understand their behaviour, or even to indicate to them that they are not the only person in the world to do this 'crazy' thing. Individuals with whom we have had contact have often searched desperately for some helpful information. More recently some useful material has been developed, but may not be as widely available as is needed (for sources see *Appendix 1*).

To suggest that workers should be aware of and open to hearing about self-injury of course implies that they are themselves adequately informed. Later in this chapter we will discuss the needs of staff for training and information.

Responding helpfully

When we are told about or encounter self-injury we are most helpful if we respond with acceptance, understanding, compassion and respect. People need first and foremost to be listened to, and taken seriously. We should endeavour to keep sight of the *person* rather than just the injury, and respond to them and to their distress as we would to anyone else.

Such a response is extremely valuable for a number of reasons:

- It encourages the person to believe that understanding and help may be possible. Perhaps her behaviour is not 'bad' or senseless, her situation is not hopeless.

'Once when I went to Casualty they seemed very ignorant and annoyed with me, but another time the nurse made me a cup of tea and sat and had a chat with me. That was really helpful. It was the first time anyone had seemed to think that there might be a real reason for my self-harm.'

- It gives a message that the person is worthwhile and deserving of care and respect. They are a whole person with many aspects to them, not just a 'self-harmer' or 'cutter'. This will help begin to counter the self-hatred and low self-esteem which contribute to the causes of self-injury.

- It provides the person with the opportunity and support to talk about her behaviour and its meanings, her difficulties and feelings. As we have seen, self-injury often functions as a 'language' in place of verbal and other forms of expression and communication. Often what self-injury communicates is the pain and confusion associated with childhood maltreatment. In some settings this material cannot be heard easily, for a variety of reasons. Where this is the case, it may be useful to turn to structured guidelines (Babiker, 1993; Cook and Babiker, 1995) that enable the creation of an environment where abuse can be spoken about with appropriate safety for all concerned.

Disapproving, condemnatory and punitive responses are not helpful, serving only to make the individual feel worse about themselves (and thus more likely to self-injure again) and to discourage them from seeking further help. Reacting in harsh or disapproving ways may briefly relieve a worker's understandable distress or frustration, but ultimately such responses are not helpful even to the person who makes them. They simply serve to interfere with communication, understanding and the development of an alliance between worker and client or patient. Meanwhile the worker may be left with uncomfortable feelings about themselves as well as about the individual concerned.

'The doctor I go to is very unhelpful – criticizes me and treats me with contempt because of my self-harm.'

Workers are sometimes worried that if they give attention to someone who self-injures they will 'reinforce' the behaviour. This is only likely to apply if the sole time the individual is heard and responded to is when she has injured herself (in which case it would make sense for her to self-injure). The answer is to listen and respond supportively to the person whether she injures herself or not, rather than to punish her for coping and expressing herself in what may, for the moment, be the only way she knows. A ward sister at a psychiatric hospital underlined this point:

'Previously I think we were reinforcing self-harm by constant observation, and the negative attitudes towards patients. We get less self-harm since we have been giving more attention to individuals and what is upsetting them.' (Arnold, 1995)

Empowerment

We have seen that many individuals who self-injure have been profoundly disempowered through their experiences of maltreatment, abandonment or oppression, and feelings of powerlessness are often dealt with through self-injury. All service users need to be treated as capable, resourceful people with rights and responsibilities for themselves. People from minority groups should have access to workers who share or at least recognize their experiences of oppression.

It is vital that services do not further disempower people, but encourage them to take charge of their own lives and development. People who injure themselves need to be allowed informed choice and control in the services and treatments they are offered. In residential or hospital settings this could include community meetings between staff and residents, in the course of which issues can be raised and decisions made. Offer and Barglow (1960) illustrate this in their finding that the most important precipitant of an outbreak of self-injury amongst young adults in their hospital study was the suspension at that time of their usual weekly community meeting.

It is not unusual for people who self-injure to be subjected to compulsory treatments. (Paradoxically, it is also common for them to be refused access to services they wish to use or discharged against their will because of self-injury.) In a review of treatments, Tantam and Whittaker (1992) conclude that compulsory psychiatric treatment is 'sometimes inescapable, that very occasionally it helps and that quite often it makes subsequent self-harm worse'.

Our suggestion is that at all times practitioners strive to work in ways which encourage individuals to take charge of their situation. This is not always easy to do, particularly where a person has already become entrenched in a passive or pathologized patient role. The giving back of control and responsibility may need to happen gradually. In all cases an important question to consider is what the approach and interventions used are teaching the person. Is there any learning taking place which will transfer usefully to life outside the service setting? For example, approaches which encourage the individual to recognize their own feelings and needs and to develop more choice about their lives and behaviour can teach important skills which the person will be able to use in supporting herself long-term.

Tackling what underlies self-injury

It is important to recognize that self-injury is often indicative of serious underlying distress and difficulties. One of the most striking findings from Arnold's (1995) research with 76 women who self-injured was their clear conviction that what they needed was help to tackle the root causes of the distress which led them to become trapped in self-injury.

The person's needs and wishes should be explored and an appropriate response or referral negotiated with them. Individual workers' own roles in relation to this will obviously vary widely. Some may be involved long-term in working at a deep level. Others may have brief or limited contact, but can be extremely helpful in responding supportively, in providing information about sorts of help available, or in making appropriate referrals to other agencies. It is always helpful to acknowledge to an individual the very painful experiences which may underlie their self-injury. However, in addressing deeper problems which may be causing self-injury, care needs to be taken only to raise as much as is safe and appropriate within the time available.

'I saw a counsellor and that helped a lot for ten weeks, but then it ended and I wasn't offered anything else. It opened up a lot of stuff which I was just left with.'

Helpful responses/services include:

- Providing ongoing opportunities for the person to express and receive support for their feelings and difficulties.
- Counselling/therapy: a supportive relationship within which the person can explore the meanings of their self-injury and address past experiences and their effects (see *Chapter 7* for a detailed discussion).
- A wide range of other therapies and approaches which facilitate exploration, expression, relaxation, self-esteem, or the fostering of a better relationship with the body. These may include arts, drama, music and dance therapies. The point is to explore and identify approaches which the individual finds appropriate and helpful.
- Group work: the opportunity to share experiences and support with others with whom one can identify (see *Chapter 6* for further discussion).
- Help with wider problems in the person's current life which may contribute to distress, such as housing, money, health, isolation, childcare, domestic violence, harassment or abuse.

The use of medication

In medical and psychiatric settings it is likely that patients will be offered drug treatments. While medication may be of value to some patients at some times, the use of this physical treatment for psychological and social difficulties is problematic, since it reinforces the very idea that lies at the root of self-injury: that is, that complex emotional or personal distress is best dealt with through immediate physical solutions.

Patients who self-injure may be dissatisfied with drug treatments, yet depend upon them in the absence of other help for their distress. In Arnold's survey many service users felt that they had been 'fobbed off' with drugs and given no opportunity to talk about their distress and the experiences underlying it. Drugs sometimes caused frightening feelings of 'unreality', confusion and inability to cope, which could lead an individual to self-injure more.

'The GP I went to didn't condemn self-injury but just ignored it, didn't ask why I did it and didn't offer me anything except anti-depressants, which didn't do anything.'

'I was just labelled and drugged up. They told me I'd be sick for life. They weren't interested in why I cut. There was no-one to talk to . . . [This] knocked the stuffing out of me.'

Tantam and Whittaker (1992) reviewed reports on use of drug treatments with people who self-injure. They conclude that 'Medication

91

carefully chosen with clear therapeutic motives and for specific symptoms may well be of value in this group of patients but there is no evidence that drugs have any direct effect on the propensity to harm the self, and considerable evidence that they are often abused, sometimes with fatal consequences'. They add that benzodiazepines tend to have a disinhibitory effect and can make self-injury worse.

In our view, drug treatments should be used only with considerable thought, and never as an alternative to dealing with the causes of a person's distress and self-injury. Patients should be fully informed about the drugs which can be offered, and, where they choose to make use of medication, involved in assessing ways in which they are helpful or unhelpful.

Responding to injuries

Clearly, workers' roles in responding to injuries will vary enormously. Where staff have a medical role in treating injuries, it is most helpful to do this kindly, calmly and respectfully, allowing the person to retain as much dignity as possible. Again, it is not helpful – nor indeed ethical – to be punitive. This is tantamount to giving the message 'you're not allowed to hurt you, but we are'.

'The treatment at my Casualty Department is unsympathetic and minimal. They ignore you, treat you as if you're just this thing to be stitched up and then shoved back out again.'

Someone who has just hurt themselves is usually upset and vulnerable, although they may hide this. The fact that they have caused the wound themselves does not mean it will not hurt, or not be frightening and shocking to them. Concern for them gives them the important message that they matter and deserve care. Again, this will not 'reinforce' self-injury unless it is the only time an individual receives any care. (Where this *is* the case, the clear need for support should be addressed, rather than the individual being condemned and punished for seeking it in the only way they currently can.)

'It never used to occur to me to take care of myself. This doctor was really gentle and comforting, and talked to me about how to look after my cuts. I find that helps me get out of a cycle – I can be nice to myself instead of just doing it worse and worse.'

Some individuals may find it helpful to be given information about caring for their own injuries and knowing when to seek medical help. It is also useful to talk to people about safety and harm-minimization. (Some of the self-help literature listed in *Appendix 1* gives information about these topics.)

It is probably preferable that those in counselling/therapy roles (including keyworkers and nurse-therapists) do not routinely also deal with a client's injuries, since this can 'muddy' the relationship. Such workers can still, however, usefully respond with concern for injuries and for the distress which has given rise to them. They may gently suggest that the person (when they feel ready) goes to someone who can treat the injuries. Staff in non-medical roles should not feel obliged to witness, deal with or hear in detail about injuries if they do not feel comfortable in doing so. It is better not to pretend, rather to be kind but matter-of-fact about one's boundaries. This should not imply any disgust for the person or their behaviour.

In most settings it is very rare for individuals to injure themselves in front of staff (unless they effectively have no privacy in which to injure). Where they do so it usually means they feel that they are not being listened to properly, and are feeling forced to communicate in a way which commands attention. In the therapeutic situation, where relational factors are often very complex, it is also very rare in our experience for the patient to attempt serious self-injury in the room with the therapist. Staff and therapist reactions to the injury in the situation may vary from a gentle suggestion to 'try to put it into words' to more definitive setting of personal boundaries, depending on the situation, and the staff member's own personal response. However this sort of incident is dealt with in the situation, it needs to be talked about and understood once the injury crisis is past. Of particular importance in this context, as we shall see in *Chapter 7*, is that the staff member or therapist's own feelings need to be explored, perhaps in supervision, and their response understood.

Attempting to stop or prevent self-injury

In our view, it is ultimately not helpful to try to stop people who wish to injure themselves from doing so. This principle can be very hard to accept. We recognize that some workers are in a position where they are required to prevent self-injury (we will discuss this situation further later). It is difficult for workers who care, or who see their role as being to protect or heal people, to stand back and let someone hurt and scar themselves. The issue however, is not whether we wish for and work towards something better for the individual, but how best this can be achieved. It is often a question of short-term versus long-term benefits. *Not* trying to stop people injuring themselves in the short term usually results in better long-term outcomes, where they are able to deal with their own difficulties and take responsibility for their own behaviour. Conversely, interfering with self-injury in the short-term (whether this is by force or persuasion) may in fact worsen their situation in the long-term, for the following reasons:

- If the person still feels the need to self-injure they will eventually find ways of doing so anyway, but more secretly and perhaps more dangerously (for example, if an individual's usual cutting implements are taken away she may use whatever she can find, clean or dirty, or may overdose or strangle herself instead).

- If the individual does not have other effective coping strategies then preventing self-injury may leave her unable to cope and more at risk of other serious harmful behaviour or even suicide.

- Trust in the professionals involved may be undermined. The alliance and communication between worker and client will suffer, particularly if the individual feels forced to lie about her self-injury.

- The person will probably also feel powerless, frightened and angry, which will lead them to need to self-injure even more. We saw in *Chapter 4* that self-injury often serves a function of allowing a person to achieve a sense of control or autonomy. Taking this away from someone will then leave them feeling even more desperate to regain some control.

- The individual's own ambivalence about their self-injury may be masked as they are forced into a polarized position. They may feel forced to identify as the 'good client' who agrees that self-injury is bad and promises not to do it (thus not acknowledging and dealing with the powerful part of themselves that wishes to injure). Alternatively, they may 'rebel' and feel even more determined to injure themselves whatever (thus losing contact with the part of themselves which wishes for change). This will seriously undermine their ability to make responsible decisions and choices about their own self-injury.

- It gives the message that the person has no rights over her own body. This reinforces a message she has probably already received as a result of abuse or oppression, and which itself plays a part in giving rise to her self-injury.

- It makes self-injury into a powerful 'weapon' or means of asserting oneself or expressing anger towards staff. This is counterproductive to any aim of making self-injury less important or compelling to the individual.

- Preventing a person injuring often effectively also stops them from talking about it. The subject becomes highly charged, or even 'taboo'. This makes it much more difficult to do the important work of co-exploring the meanings and functions of self-injury for the individual.

- Some of the measures commonly adopted to try to control self-injury amongst clients can be oppressive and damaging. These can include: compulsory admission to hospital and treatment with drugs against their will; placing individuals under continuous observation; searching and confiscating their possessions; physical restraint; the use of 'token economies' or the granting and withholding of 'privileges'; in secure environments, putting individuals into strip cells; excluding clients from therapeutic services if they self-injure; and requiring them to enter into 'contracts' or promises undertaking not to self-injure. This can make individuals feel that they are 'bad', out of control, and not capable of being responsible for themselves. This is not conducive to real growth and change. The emotional harm which such actions may do to the person (especially given the likelihood that at least some of them will be reminiscent of childhood abuse) needs to be weighed against the damage which the person's continued self-injury may do. In many cases, the injuries involved are not severe and the means used to prevent them are unjustifiably intrusive, dehumanising or infantilising. Staff themselves may also feel distressed and uncomfortable about the roles they feel obliged to take with patients.

'The consultant said we had to just ignore a patient when she cut herself, we shouldn't talk to her, then she'd stop it. We didn't agree but we did it. It was horrible.'

'Sometimes I feel like an abuser. I wonder which is worse, them cutting themselves or us grabbing them and stopping them.'

In suggesting that workers should not try to prevent someone hurting themselves, we are not in any sense advocating that they adopt an attitude of indifference to self-injury. They do not have to pretend that it is fine to carry on harming oneself. In fact it could be very hurtful to the person injuring themselves to imply that we do not care what happens to their bodies. In our view, the most helpful approach is one which combines understanding of the survival value of self-injury, with concern for the person's physical safety and support for their efforts to move towards other means of coping and expressing themselves. Workers can accept that at the moment the person sometimes needs to injure themselves, while exploring with them ways they can minimize the damage done and care for their bodies as best as possible. They can respect the importance to them of self-injury and its meanings, while encouraging the development of other ways of supporting and expressing themselves.

Some staff work in contexts where they have responsibilities which are not consistent with a completely 'non-interventionist' approach to self-injury. However, it is important to be realistic about this. Fear of accountability can lead workers to panic unnecessarily about quite minor self-injury. It is for managers to establish exactly what their agency's responsibilities are and to incorporate these into clear guidelines for staff. Such guidelines could also cover any necessary risk assessment procedures.

Where staff feel that they *must* intervene in a person's self-injury, it is important to try to ensure that their patients or clients can retain the maximum possible dignity and responsibility for themselves. Most people, given the chance and an explanation, will understand the position of a worker or agency with responsibility and concern for their safety. Many will be willing to negotiate with workers in order to keep their self-injury within acceptable limits. They may be willing to accept certain restrictions, if they have a say in these. And they can be invited to suggest ways in which staff can best support them in their efforts to cope without injuring themselves. At all times, the long-term aim can be kept in mind of equipping the individual to *keep themselves safe*, rather than encouraging them to hand over responsibility for their safety to others.

Support

Many people who self-injure have at times a great need for emotional support. Some find it hard to reach out for and accept support, while others may make great use of many services in their search for support. The need may increase for a while during stressful periods, or when a person is exploring experiences underlying their self-injury. As well as ongoing, reliable, regular support, people often need access to help in a crisis – someone to talk to, to phone or somewhere to go to be safe when they feel overwhelmed. At such times people need to be allowed time to talk in an unpressured, exploratory way, since they do not always know immediately what is causing their distress.

It is helpful if agencies can be flexible in providing levels and types of support appropriate to people's needs at different times. They can also have up-to-date information available about other sources of support in the area. Support should not only be given or increased in response to self-injury, nor should it be conditional on not injuring, as such approaches merely reinforce the significance and power of self-injury. In addressing someone's support needs it is again crucial to allow clients or patients to retain responsibility and self-respect. A delicate balance may need to be struck between making sure enough support is available so that the person can cope, yet not taking over and disempowering them. It is important to work out with the individual how to access support when needed, whilst both parties keep sight of and work to develop the person's own strengths and resources. Over time, those working with an individual can help them to identify the kinds of situations which are likely to lead to them becoming overwhelmed and self-injury occurring or escalating, and to plan for ways of supporting themselves and accessing environmental support.

Institutional factors affecting self-injury

It is important to consider how the institution in which staff work and/or the behaviour of staff (and other service-users) may be implicated in individuals' self-injury. Since self-injury is functional and meaningful (see *Chapter 4*), it follows that it may serve important functions in relation to the institution or helping relationship as well as to the individual's life outside. It is not unusual for self-injury to be triggered or to escalate in response to factors *within* a service setting. Where this may be happening, general questions to be considered include:

- Are service users/clients being made to feel helpless, vulnerable and controlled?
- Is self-injury the only circumstance under which people are taken seriously and listened to?
- Are service users being harassed, oppressed or assaulted (by other clients or staff)?
- Is self-injury the only available means of expressing distress and anger or of releasing tension?
- Are unresolved staff conflicts affecting service users? (As we saw in *Chapter 1*, there is evidence that staff conflict may be related to escalation in self-injury amongst those in institutional settings, Aldridge, 1988.)
- Is self-injury the sole means of achieving certain desired ends, such as providing the only opportunity for a change of environment or for attention to safety or health?
- Are service-users bored, understimulated or isolated? (This applies mainly in residential and institutional settings.)
- Is self-injury the only means of expressing dissatisfaction with staff or with aspects of the environment or service?
- Is the culture of the client group being allowed to operate in some way to foster self-injury, perhaps as a norm or means of belonging?
- In what ways does the institution replicate the cultural context – with regard to gender, race, sexual orientation and so on – in which individuals may develop self-injury? How may this affect service users? (See *Chapter 3* for a full discussion of this issue.)

Others affected by self-injury

Self-injury on the part of an individual may have considerable impact on other service users, as well as on families and friends. It may cause great distress, anger and anxiety. In turn, these other people may react to the self-injury in ways which are hurtful and unhelpful to the individual concerned. Workers may therefore need to find ways of supporting other service-users and perhaps family members/friends who are upset by self-injury. They may also need to protect individuals who self-injure from denigration and ridicule.

Workers can help by providing information about self-injury so that others affected are more able to understand the behaviour (see *Appendix 1* for resources). It may be necessary to talk through the issue and the feelings it arouses with the people concerned. Family members may need to be referred to other sources of support for themselves. It may also be helpful to discuss with the individual who is injuring themselves whether there are some reasonable ways in which the impact of the behaviour on others could be mitigated. In some settings it is appropriate to discuss self-injury with a group, perhaps broadening the discussion to include other forms of 'self-harm' which group members may engage in, or ways of coping which people employ. In settings where other clients may be affected by the demands made on staff by those who self-injure, staffing levels should be adequate to respond to the needs of all service-users. Those who self-injure should not be scapegoated for the demands they make on staff time.

Support for Effective Working

We saw in *Chapter 1* that self-injury can be one of the most difficult behaviours for professionals (and supporters) to cope with, frequently arousing very strong and uncomfortable reactions. Workers report feeling a range of powerful emotions when faced with self-injury, including horror, sadness, powerlessness, anger and frustration. They may feel responsible, yet inadequate to help, and perhaps afraid that their response will somehow make someone's self-injury worse.

The difficulties staff experience are frequently compounded by lack of training and information about self-injury and by the absence of explicit policies, guidelines and support for dealing with it. If workers are to be able to respond effectively to clients who self-injure, and to come through in a healthy manner themselves, their needs for training, guidance and support must be recognised and addressed.

Training

Many professionals working in agencies and roles where they come into frequent contact with people who self-injure have received little or no training on the subject. This leaves them feeling anxious, distressed and unsure how to understand and deal with self-injury when they encounter it.

❘Training about self-injury needs to take place both as part of initial professional training and later in an in-service context.❘Here it is often particularly useful for staff working in teams within an agency to attend training together, enabling discussion of their particular concerns and dilemmas. The precise content of this training needs to be determined as appropriate to the agency and the roles of staff concerned. Some or all of the following topics may be important:

Information about self-injury

Workers need basic information about the nature of self-injury and its relationship to (and differences from) suicide attempts and other self-harming and/or violent behaviours.

Attitudes and feelings about self-injury

It is valuable for staff to have the opportunity to identify and discuss their feelings and concerns about self-injury and clients who self-injure, and how these impact on their work. They will then be better able to make rational decisions about how to respond to self-injury in their work setting. Staff teams may also identify their own needs for support, back-up and/or supervision in this work.

Why people self-injure

Staff need an understanding of the functional nature of self-injury and of the life experiences and feelings which tend to underlie this behaviour. This allows them to feel less mystified and inadequate when faced with someone who self-injures, and to determine more appropriate ways of working with individuals.

Responding to people who self-injure

Training should explore the needs of people who self-injure and provide information about what is helpful and unhelpful in responding to them. Workers in different roles will need varying levels of information about treatment models, but all will benefit from information about service users' views on what is helpful, as well as the experience of other professionals. Teams undergoing training together can then consider the implications of this information for work in their own setting.

Agency policies and guidelines

Where an agency has a policy (or some sort of defined approach) for dealing with self-injury, training can provide teams with an opportunity to learn about and to review this, exchanging honest views as to how useful and workable it is for staff and clients. Where no policy or guidelines for dealing with self-injury exist (as is common), training can provide an impetus and opportunity for staff to begin identifying the need for these and the issues they should cover.

Specific responsibilities concerning self-injury

Staff in different settings may be required to carry out various particular roles and tasks with respect to self-injury, and may need training on these. Such responsibilities and tasks include risk assessment; care planning; harm reduction/prevention; and so on.

The impact of self-injury on others

Many staff will be in the position of working with fellow service-users or families of people who self-injure. They will benefit from the opportunity in training to consider the impact of self-injury on such others and the most helpful ways of informing and supporting them in coping with this. Managers undergoing training should also be given the opportunity to consider the impact of self-injury on staff and their needs for back-up, support and supervision.

Resources

Training courses should provide information about relevant local and national services for people who self-injure, useful literature and interest/support networks for those working in this and related areas (see *Appendix 1*).

Policies and Procedures

Few agencies have any clearly defined policy on dealing with self-injury. This means that staff are left to flounder. Their responses to self-injury may be founded on inadequate information, or on impressions they have picked up about how self-injury is dealt with. There may be variations in responses to self-injury between different staff, so that clients feel anxious and may try to play staff off against each other. Different clients may also be treated differently, which can be confusing, distressing and divisive. In the absence of policy and guidance, staff are likely to become more concerned with 'watching their own backs', at the expense of consideration of their clients' needs for such things as privacy, choice and responsibility.

On the other hand, a well thought-out policy and guidance on dealing with self-injury can support and free staff to work confidently and creatively. Such policy and guidelines need to be worked out by groups comprising representatives of staff from all levels/ disciplines who will be expected to work within them, together or in consultation with service users or their representatives.

Examples of the sorts of things which a policy and associated procedures and guidelines may need to cover are:

- The organization's understanding of and philosophy concerning self-injury and its own role and responsibilities in respect of this.
- Any rules concerning admission to/use of the service by people who self-injure.
- Confidentiality and any circumstances under which confidentiality may be breached with respect to injury.
- Responding – to injuries themselves and/or to disclosure of self-injury.
- Safety, including such issues as health and safety for staff and service users; access to first aid equipment; clients' access to objects which may be used for self-injury; harm-reduction measures.
- Intervention/prevention: whether to, under which circumstances, and how staff may or should intervene or act to prevent self-injury.
- Training, information, supervision and support available to staff dealing with self-injury.
- Recording and reporting requirements.

Support

All workers having significant contact with people who self-injure need support (as well as possibly more formal supervision – see *Chapter 7* for a fuller discussion). Support is not a luxury, but an important basis for effective and professional working. It is our experience that few workers feel they have adequate support, and they recognize that they themselves as well as their work with clients suffer as a result. Lack of funds and time are usually cited as the reasons for this inadequacy. There is a clear need for agencies to pay greater attention to the support needs of staff and to be creative in finding ways of responding to these, even where resources are limited.

Precisely what forms of support are needed will vary according to the person's particular role, but elements of what is needed may include some or all of the following:

- **Contact with other workers:** some professionals work alone or have little chance to spend time with colleagues. At the very least workers need opportunities to meet and be with others who share similar work.

- **Offloading:** opportunities to let off steam, to talk about the difficult issues and feelings which are being brought up by working with self-injury. (This may sometimes lead to the recognition that a worker needs further support to tackle distress of their own which is being triggered by work with clients.)

- **Recognition:** acknowledgement and appreciation for the difficulties being tackled and the efforts and progress being made.

- **Sharing ideas:** the chance to discuss the work with others, bouncing around ideas and gaining new insights.

- **Support in the work itself:** in situations where a client needs a high level of contact and care it is probably best if other people can share the load.

- **Back-up:** staff working with people who self-injure need to know that they are backed by their colleagues, and, most importantly, by their managers. Staff need to be able to call on others for advice and support. They are operating in an area of risk and they need to know that they will not be scapegoated or left to 'carry the can' alone if clients in their care continue to self-injure, or indeed come to significant harm.

Some possible ways of providing these elements include the following.

Teamworking

Responsibility for working with clients who self-injure may most usefully be shared within small multi-disciplinary teams. These will benefit by regularly planning and reviewing their work together, and can provide each other with on-going support.

'Sometimes you visit someone, and when you leave you don't know whether they are going to hurt themselves before you next see them. It helps to be able to talk to other people who know them and have to take risks like that too.'

Supervision

We discuss supervision for therapy and counselling in more depth in *Chapter 7*. Here we wish to stress the supervision needs of staff who are not engaged in ongoing counselling or therapy, but whose roles involve providing significant levels of support and care for people who self-injure. Such workers need a supportive space to reflect on their work and, importantly, on their own feelings and responses and the ways these impact on their work with clients. Supervision needs to be given importance and time. It is often preferable if it can be provided by someone who is not the worker's line manager, so that the situation is not 'muddied' by concerns about appraisal or case management. Group or peer arrangements may be means of providing useful supervision at reasonable cost (Arnold and Magill, 1996).

Regular staff/team meetings

It is valuable for staff groups and teams to meet together regularly, within work time, to share support and discuss issues of concern. When self-injury among the client group is a major issue, the character of these meetings becomes very important. It can be helpful to appoint an informal 'facilitator' for each meeting who will ensure that the group maintains its focus on staff support, rather than drifting into general or anecdotal talk.

Where time is a problem it is important to be creative. It is often more possible than first appears for staff groups to take time out for such meetings. For example, on one specialist unit for people who self-injure severely, the whole staff team takes an hour away from patients each day, trusting patients to be able to take responsibility and support one another in their absence.

Peer support groups

A variation on the previous idea is to set up smaller groups of people, not necessarily those from the same team, who wish to meet together for mutual support around a particular theme such as self-injury. Multi-agency interest and support groups can also be helpful, particularly for those working in settings where they are isolated, or where others do not share their perspective on issues such as self-injury.

6. Working in Particular Settings with People who Self-Injure

In this chapter we draw on the principles discussed in *Chapter 5* to develop ideas about working with people who self-injure in a range of community and institutional/residential settings. Clearly, we cannot discuss every setting in which staff may encounter self-injury, but we hope that our coverage of those we do address specifically will offer all readers some ideas of interest and relevance to their own workplace. Those engaged in therapy and counselling with clients will also find more detailed discussion of issues concerning their work in *Chapter 7*.

Community Settings

Many community-based (statutory, voluntary and independent) agencies are likely to number amongst their users individuals who self-injure (yet they may not always be made aware of this behaviour). Here we concentrate on the issues arising within primary care settings, accident and emergency departments, community mental health services, and voluntary sector support and helpline projects. We also consider the role of support groups, which may of course be found in a range of settings.

Primary care settings

A General Practitioner's (GP's) surgery or health centre is often the first port of call for someone seeking help for self-injury, or (perhaps more commonly) for the psychological distress underlying self-injury. GPs are in a good position to pick up self-injury early, in children as well as adults, and to arrange for appropriate help to be provided.

There is a variety of ways in which self-injury may come to the attention of a GP or Practice Nurse. Rarely, patients may talk openly about what they are doing to themselves. Staff may also see evidence of possible self-injury during examinations and medical procedures. Gentle enquiry and a supportive response may be needed to help a person to be truthful about their injuries. Disclosure may also come from the family of the person who self-injures, rather than from the person themselves.

In the UK a GP is the main referral agent, and frequently now also the source of funds for treatment, so their response to a large extent determines a patient's chances of getting access to appropriate help. Many people who self-injure say that what they need is the opportunity to talk through and resolve the causes of their difficulties in a non-pathologizing context (Arnold, 1995). GPs need to be aware of a range of possibilities for referral (including non-statutory services), and to discuss options respectfully with their patient. Increasing numbers of GP surgeries now employ a Practice Counsellor, and a patient may find such counselling valuable and less stigmatizing than attendance at a hospital or mental health resource. However, where such counselling is available only on a short-term basis, it may not be appropriate for patients who have suffered severely traumatic experiences and need longer-term therapy.

GPs and other primary care professionals may have a long-standing relationship with a patient, and are usually local and available. This means that they can provide a degree of flexible, ongoing or crisis support which can help a person who self-injures to cope outside of hospital.

'My GP has been very accepting and supportive; he spends time and listens to me. Sometimes when I have been feeling unsafe I've been able to go there at the end of surgery – just to have someone to check in with, who cares whether I'm alive or dead.'

GPs and Practice Nurses can also help a person who self-injures practically, by teaching them how to take care of their injuries, and talking to them about how to keep themselves reasonably safe. (Many patients would prefer for their injuries to be dealt with at their GP's surgery where possible, rather than going to the Accident and Emergency Department at their hospital.)

Where the partner and/or family of a person who self-injures attends the same practice, staff may have an important role to play in supporting others who are extremely distressed and frightened by an individual's self-injury. A GP may also be subject to pressure from the family to stop the person's self-injury, and will need to help them understand and cope with the fact that this is not usually possible, at least in the short term. Primary care workers may be well placed to pick up any problems in a relationship or family, and may also have important knowledge about the practical and economic circumstances of patients, all of which may be relevant to the distress of the person who is injuring themselves. This may be important in determining who needs help, and of what kind.

Accident and Emergency Departments

Along with GPs, those working in Accident and Emergency (A and E) settings are likely to be amongst the first professionals an individual may approach in relation to self-injury. They therefore need to be alert to the possibility that some injuries they see will be self-inflicted, and be prepared to respond with sensitivity and acceptance.

Many staff working in this area feel that A and E is an inappropriate setting for 'psychiatric emergencies', including self-injury. (This raises the important issue of the general lack of crisis support for people in emotional distress, especially out-of-hours, in many areas.) A and E departments are frequently busy and staff may feel they do not have the time or training to respond as fully as they might wish to someone in acute emotional distress. The difficulties for staff are compounded by the fact that, unlike a GP, they will usually have had little or no previous contact or relationship with the patient. The one-off, brief nature of their contact means their role is frustratingly limited and staff may feel that there is very little they can do to deal with a patient's real needs. On the other hand, the same patient may present themselves for treatment repeatedly, in which case staff can become frustrated, disillusioned and angry.

Users of A and E often have very different perceptions and expectations of the service from those of the staff. A and E is usually the only face-to-face service which is available 24 hours per day and to which there is immediate, open access, without referral. This means that people who self-injure may see their local A and E department as a potential lifeline. As well as seeking medical treatment, people attending for self-inflicted injuries may be feeling in desperate need of support. Women responding to the research project at Bristol Crisis Service for Women (Arnold, 1995) acknowledged that they might sometimes, when desperate, injure themselves just so that they could have a 'valid' reason for making contact with someone who might help them, usually at A and E.

'I wish you could sometimes just go there when you need to talk and be safe, without having to harm yourself first.'

There is, then, a disparity between the nature of the service available at A and E departments, and the complex motivations and needs of some patients attending. This can lead to disappointment and frustration for both patients and staff. Many staff are aware that patients may want more support from them than they feel able to provide, and some react to their frustration (and perhaps guilt) by becoming angry and critical towards the patient who makes such 'unreasonable' demands.

A patient attending A and E following an incident of self-injury may be shocked and upset. This, together with anxiety about revealing their self-injury may make them uncommunicative, defensive or sometimes aggressive. Staff themselves may feel shocked or distressed by seeing self-inflicted injuries. On the other hand, even where a person is in acute distress their injuries may be quite superficial, leaving staff feeling their time is being wasted on trivia. The difficult life experiences and feelings which have given rise to the self-injury (and which might otherwise have evoked some understanding and empathy from staff) may not be known or apparent. User organizations (Pembroke, 1994; 1996) have suggested that individuals who self-injure could carry a crisis card, recognized by hospital staff, which gives some explanation of their situation and needs.

Arnold's survey of users' experience of services found that, whilst some had at times good experiences of attendance at A and E, many had received harsh or even punitive treatment. This included criticism and verbal abuse, being kept waiting longer than other patients for treatment and being sutured without local anaesthetic. Some women who self-injured repeatedly had been refused necessary treatment altogether, some felt their treatment was inadequate, whilst for others treatment for injuries was conditional on their agreeing to see the duty psychiatrist.

'Once when I went the doctor was really caring, and said he would stitch my cuts so they would hardly scar. Another time a doctor really hurt me, and hardly bothered. I had a lot of trouble with that wound healing.'

A and E departments need to develop policy and guidelines on responding to self-injury, in consultation with user groups. Such policy should cover the way in which staff treat the person's physical injuries (including such issues as waiting time, pain relief and privacy), and should also provide guidance as to the understanding of self-injury and the attitude to be taken towards patients. (Detailed recommendations for the treatment of patients who self-injure have been drawn up by the National Self-harm Network – see references in *Appendix 1*.)

There is also the need to examine systematically how the non-medical needs of people who self-injure should be dealt with. Some A and E departments routinely refer patients who have harmed themselves in any way to the psychiatrist on duty, while others do this only in the case of apparent suicide attempts. In the case of self-injury, a more flexible policy on referral would be most helpful, with patients being asked what their own needs and wishes are. For some people who self-injure, referral to a psychiatrist may provide an important opportunity to obtain access to help for their underlying difficulties. However, many people do not want to see a psychiatrist when attending A and E, although they may want some emotional support. Consideration could be given to other means of providing this, perhaps by nursing staff (when available) or by volunteers. We are aware of some hospitals which have responded to the problem by linking with community mental health services or with local voluntary organizations. These provide part-time counselling support services within A and E Departments. Whilst such arrangements can be of great value, it is important that they do not result in A and E staff feeling that they themselves have no role in providing emotional support to patients. For although it may seem to staff working in A and E departments that they are not in a position to provide anything to someone who self-injures, other than repeated 'patching-up', in fact they can offer help of considerable value. Kindness, acceptance and listening can encourage the person to feel a little better about themselves, and to believe it may be worth seeking further help. Staff can also provide information on other services (both statutory and non-statutory) in the area.

Community Mental Health Settings

This section concerns statutory community mental health teams and day hospital (or resource centre) settings. These are usually multidisciplinary and can potentially provide an extremely valuable service to people struggling with self-injury and the distress underlying it. They may be able to offer a variety of therapeutic approaches and types of support flexibly over an extended period, as appropriate to the needs of the client. They can support an individual in coping with life in the community, without the need for in-patient treatment and the disempowerment and stigmatization which can accompany this. Early referrals to community services may provide an opportunity for appropriate help to be offered to an individual before their distress and self-injury become so acute and entrenched as to lead to repeated hospital admissions.

'My CPN came out to me every evening for a while, and we talked for a bit. It got me through to the next day, when I was really desperate.'

Unfortunately, however, lack of resources can often mean that the services cannot fulfil their real potential in responding to the needs of people who self-injure (nor indeed to other patients). In the UK, recent measures limiting the provision of mental health services to those suffering 'severe mental illness' has meant that proactive or preventative work is less common. Often neither self-injury alone nor the traumatic experiences which underlie it are regarded as sufficiently severe problems to warrant provision of mental health services. This is frustrating and distressing for staff, and means that some individuals have to continue to somehow endure their distress and self-injury without support. In some cases, the lack of help allows their condition to deteriorate, until they reach a state where they do fit the criteria of 'mental illness' and so qualify for services. It is extremely regrettable that community mental health services should be prevented from responding more flexibly to the needs and distress of those who self-injure, without pathologizing them.

Where patients are offered a service, this is often time-limited, with pressure on staff to bring about observable improvement in an individual's condition and to discharge them within a short time – perhaps a few weeks or months. For some individuals, short-term work may be very valuable; however, self-injury tends often to be a long-term problem. Resolving the experiences which underlie self-injury (such as abuse) often requires work over a period of some years. Limiting the service offered to a short period may mean that the opportunity is lost of providing real help which will bring about lasting improvement. The requirement for 'observable' outcomes can put pressure on workers to try to stop an individual's self-injury before the person is truly ready to cope without it. Where this is unsuccessful they may become impatient and frustrated with their client.

Other issues concerning work with self-injury in community mental health settings may include the following.

- The possible involvement of staff in compulsory hospital admissions or treatment orders. Where a good relationship has been built up, a worker may be in a very good position to make a realistic assessment of an individual's condition and needs, and to negotiate with their client what support and treatment are appropriate. On the other hand, their possible role in decisions concerning compulsory treatment may interfere with the development of a therapeutic alliance with clients. This may also prevent clients from contacting a service when feeling in need of support in a crisis.

'I wish I could talk to someone without having to worry about being sectioned. Sometimes I really need help but I daren't say what's going on with me.'

- There is a great need and demand for counselling amongst people who injure themselves (Arnold, 1995), and it is to be welcomed that community psychiatric nurses (CPNs) are increasingly taking a counselling role with patients, so long as they are trained and supervised for this. However, thought needs to be given to the possible conflicts between counselling and other treatment roles. It is difficult for a patient to feel safe in a counselling relationship with someone who also gives her injections (perhaps into her bottom), especially if she would prefer not to be receiving such drug treatment. The situation is exacerbated if the CPN is male (as is often the case) and the patient a woman who has experienced abuse as a child (again, often the case with someone who self-injures). Such roles should be separated.

- Staff working in the community with someone who self-injures may experience considerable anxiety about their client's safety. They may leave someone after visiting feeling concerned that they may injure themselves before they are next able to visit, perhaps severely. They may have to make difficult judgements about risk. Staff in this position need back-up and support.

- There may be little or no out-of-hours provision for clients in distress or crisis. Community mental health workers are often only too aware that their service is not available at times when clients may be at their most vulnerable (such as evenings and weekends). This can lead to unplanned and perhaps avoidable hospital admissions. There is a clear need for more provision for flexible, easily accessible and non-stigmatizing emergency support. Community teams in a few areas have set up out-of-hours telephone (and face to face) support services to try to address this problem. In other cases, it is helpful for workers to provide clients with information about other local resources providing support.

- There is a need for good communication and liaison both within teams where more than one member is working with a client, and between community teams and other professionals involved with clients, such as GPs and hospital staff. Without this it is possible that workers may take different and perhaps contradictory approaches to an individual's self-injury. Clients may feel confused and their confidence in their treatment may be undermined. An unhelpful situation may also be set up where a client is able to override the decisions made by one worker by approaching another who has not been adequately informed. Keyworker systems should be able to avoid such situations, as long as all professionals involved with a client are fully informed and co-operate with the arrangement.

- To the extent that community mental health services and day hospitals reflect an 'illness' model of psychological distress and its treatment, some of the issues which we will discuss later in respect of psychiatric in-patient settings may be relevant. These include the possibility that people can become disempowered and identified with a passive 'sick' role. As with in-patient services, an approach which allows patients to retain dignity, responsibility and choice is to be preferred.

Voluntary Sector Support Services and Helplines

Voluntary sector agencies which are likely to be contacted by people who self-injure include those concerned with rape and sexual abuse, domestic violence, suicide, emotional/mental health crisis, young people at risk, and so on. A very wide range of types of service may be offered, including drop-in support and information/advice services, counselling, advocacy and helplines. In theory, such services can be extremely flexible in responding appropriately to users' needs, since they are independent and not so subject to limiting criteria for referral and so on as statutory service providers. In many cases, unfortunately, this flexibility has been undermined by restrictions in and conditions on funding. At the same time, voluntary agencies in the UK have in recent years found greater numbers of more severely distressed individuals with more severe problems (including self-injury) approaching their services. If statutory mental health services are to be increasingly limited and are to provide lower levels of support to smaller numbers of people, voluntary services which pick up their former patients need to be properly funded on a long-term and consistent basis. This is essential to enable them to plan and implement appropriate services, and to properly support staff and volunteers.

Voluntary agencies' services may be particularly attractive to people who self-injure, for a number of reasons. Their non-statutory, independent position can make them feel safer for individuals who are afraid that they may be compulsorily admitted to hospital or that their children may be taken into care if their self-injury becomes known to statutory services. Others (especially those who are themselves health workers) may be afraid to approach statutory services because of concern for their careers. Some services (particularly helplines but also drop-in and other services) can be used without the need to give names and personal details. This assurance of anonymity can be attractive to individuals who feel ashamed of their self-injury.

Users of voluntary services may find them far less disempowering than psychiatric services. In many cases, voluntary sector agencies are able to provide services which are quickly and easily accessible, without the need for formal referral and assessment processes. Organizations may be user-managed or led and may employ staff and volunteers who are open about their own experiences of emotional distress, abuse and so on. This may be particularly important to users who feel they have been harshly or inappropriately treated or stigmatized by statutory mental health services, and they may feel that such people offer greater understanding and empathy.

'It is helpful to know someone will listen to you and not treat you as a freak or be totally gobsmacked if you say "I've just cut".'

Helpline services can be particularly valuable for individuals who self-injure, and staff working on many types of helpline need to be prepared to encounter and support such callers. It is reassuring for callers who fear being condemned for self-injury to feel that they can try out the contact briefly and then put the phone down if the response is not sympathetic. Many helplines are available at times when people are likely to feel particularly low and isolated and likely to injure themselves, such as at night and weekends, when other services are not usually open. Access may be available instantly, when the person feels sufficient courage or desperation to seek help. A helpline may be the first service contacted by a person who self-injures, or in which their self-injury is disclosed. Some may feel encouraged by this contact to go on to seek face-to-face help. Other people may not feel able to contact any other service, and may rely on one or more helplines as their sole source of help. Some people use helplines only intermittently, when feeling particularly distressed, others use them as a source of regular and long-term support. People who self-injure are particularly likely to telephone a helpline at times when they feel the desire to hurt themselves but do not want to act on this, or when they feel at risk of particularly severe self-injury. Some may also ring for support following an incident of self-injury which has left them feeling ashamed, frightened or upset.

'I was experiencing a very strong urge to self-harm prior to the call. This had gone by the end of the call, by working out why and what to do instead.'
(Lindsay, 1995)

Telephone helplines have a number of limitations. It can be very hard for a caller to trust the counsellor and to feel they are receiving empathy and support when communication is restricted to voices on the telephone. The one-off, unplanned nature of each contact can be difficult for both callers and workers, as there is usually little opportunity for callers to build up a relationship with a telephone

counsellor. This may mean that they feel unable to disclose important material, or that they do so, but subsequently feel frightened,
exposed and unsupported. Some helplines do have provision for
callers to plan calls to a specific worker with whom they can build
up a relationship, but this is not often possible.

*'When you're feeling upset and vulnerable it's very scary to pick up the
phone and ask for help when you have no idea who is going to be on the
other end. What if they're horrible to you, or just don't understand? They
don't know you – how can they care about you?'*

Some helplines are very heavily used and callers have to be extremely persistent to get through. Someone in distress may feel let down
and disheartened if they repeatedly hear an engaged tone, and have
no idea when or whether their call will be successful. Helplines may
need greater and more predictable funding to meet potential users'
needs. Again, there is a clear need for funders and purchasers to
recognize the value of the services provided by voluntary agencies
and to support them adequately.

Support Groups

Support groups may be offered within a very wide range of agencies, or may be independent or set up on a self-help basis. Group
work can be very helpful at the right time, and in our experience,
individuals are often keen to take part in groups with others who
self-injure, or who share other aspects of their experience (such as
childhood abuse). Some workers are wary of allowing people who
self-injure to take part in group work together, usually due to concern that members will encourage and copy one another's self-
injury. In our experience such concerns are generally unfounded, so
long as groups are well set up and supported.

Some of the particular benefits which individuals may experience
from taking part in a group include:

- reducing isolation and secrecy;
- acceptance, identification and a reduction in feelings of being
  'different' or 'wrong';
- developing self-understanding through understanding others in
  the group;
- new experiences of mutual respect, trust, empathy and intimacy;
- developing communication skills;
- an opportunity to observe, share and learn ways of expressing
  and coping with feelings;

113

- experiencing oneself as able to offer something to others, to draw on one's negative experience in order to be helpful and supportive to other group members;
- empowerment: experiencing feelings of solidarity and strength as a member of a group. A group setting also often allows members to feel a far greater degree of equality, control and mutuality than is possible in individual therapy.

Groups also have certain limitations, which may make them inappropriate for some individuals at some times. In particular, there is unlikely to be time every meeting for every member to be fully heard or for their individual needs to be met. Members who are feeling particularly distressed and fragile may feel overwhelmed by hearing of others' experiences. Group members may also themselves experience many of the reactions which workers experience to others' disclosures about self-injury (or trauma). For groups to be beneficial and effective they must be well supported, with clear and consistent boundaries which enable members to feel safe and contained (Arnold and Magill, 1996).

Working in Residential, In-Patient and Secure Settings with People who Self-Injure

There is a wide range of residential and institutional settings in which staff may find themselves working with people who self-injure. We begin by discussing in depth a range of common issues which may need to be dealt with in many different residential/institutional settings. We go on to examine some particular issues which arise in the specific settings of in-patient psychiatric units and secure environments respectively.

Common issues within residential, in-patient and secure settings

Responsibility for residents' safety

Within residential, in-patient and institutional (including secure) settings there is often particular concern about responsibility and accountability with respect to self-inflicted injury. The agency may also be subject to expectations from referring agents and clients' families that they will prevent individuals from hurting themselves.

The result of this is that staff may fear they will be vulnerable to blame or even legal action if someone in their care injures themselves in any way, however minor. It may be difficult for them to reconcile these concerns about responsibility and accountability with their clients' needs for autonomy, privacy and responsibility for themselves. Those working in non-statutory environments may feel that they carry considerable responsibility, but without the accompanying authority and access to other services which are available to those in environments run by medical/psychiatric and social services. (Good communication with, and support from, referring/funding agents is very important in this as in many other respects.) As discussed in *Chapter 5*, staff need to be well briefed and supported in respect of responsibility and risk, otherwise they may 'play safe' and adopt an overly authoritarian approach to a client with a history of self-injury.

Supporting a resident who self-injures

Where someone who self-injures is to join a residential or in-patient setting, planning is very valuable. Staffing levels should be adequate (and flexible enough) to support all residents, even where self-injury imposes extra demands. Where possible, it is a good idea for any prospective resident to visit in advance and to talk through what their needs and wants are in relation to self-injury, amongst other things. Staff can also explain any policy on self-injury, and they can explore how best the client and staff can work together. This can also be done on and following admission. Residents' confidence in identifying and asserting their needs will grow as they become comfortable in the placement, while their needs in relation to support will also change over time.

Support needs (emotional, practical and social) may be very high, at least at times. It is important that a resident who self-injures knows what support is available to them, especially when they are distressed. It helps greatly if people know that there are regular and reliable opportunities for them to talk with a worker about their feelings and experiences – such as planned sessions with a keyworker. A resident who self-injures also needs to be able to ask for support at moments of crisis. Residential settings theoretically have the greatest potential for providing appropriate levels of support to meet individuals' changing needs. However, while some may be understaffed, in other units aspects of staff's roles (for example, in respect of discipline or management) may be incompatible with providing the emotional support and perhaps in-depth therapeutic work a person needs. There may be a need to employ the services of individual workers or agencies from outside the residential environment in order to provide support within appropriate boundaries. In some instances (especially, but not exclusively, in hospital environments) the nature and extent of support offered may be infantilizing and disempowering to service users, who need to be encouraged to have a greater say in determining their true support needs.

Effects of self-injury on other service-users

Within a residential or institutional setting the emotional atmosphere may often be highly charged, with service users routinely witnessing considerable distress. In addition, any self-injury on the part of service users is likely to happen on the premises. It is therefore likely to be upsetting and disruptive to other patients and residents, who may feel frightened, responsible, angry or jealous of the concern which self-injury evokes. In some instances self-injury may lead to a general atmosphere of unpredictability, anxiety and chaos, which is very unhelpful to vulnerable clients (Pawlicki and Gaumer, 1993). They may react to their feelings by rejecting and ridiculing the person who self-injures, or sometimes by beginning to hurt themselves.

Some residential projects involve existing residents in meetings concerning admission of new people. In any event, it is a good idea to talk with existing residents or patients about self-injury. This can help them to accept, cope with and support a new resident who self-injures. In order to feel safe in what is effectively (if temporarily) their home, residents need to know that staff can handle self-injury. They may need reassurance that staff will be available to them and will not see them as less upset or important than a person who hurts themselves.

The role of the institution with respect to the occurrence of self-injury

Sometimes individuals who have no history of self-injury begin to injure themselves following admission to hospital, prison or residential facility. Others may self-injure more or less severely than usual when in a residential setting. Consideration needs to be given to factors within the placement which may influence self-injury. Self-injury may also occur in 'rashes'. Where a number of clients self-injure an element of copying or competition between them may appear to be operating.

Staff may try to deal with what they see as 'contagion' (or competitiveness) by various means. These may include separating individuals who self-injure from one another, or alternatively segregating groups of clients who self-injure from other residents. Various attempts at behaviour modification may be made. In some units peer pressure is used, with individuals who self-injure being required to account for themselves to a meeting of residents, who then decide what sanction should be applied.

In our view there are several possible reasons for any onset or escalation of self-injury following admission. For some individuals, self-injury may be a response to feelings of anxiety, loss, distress, disorientation, powerlessness, and many other feelings induced by being away from home and in a strange environment. Individuals may not have access to their normal supports and means of expressing or coping with their feelings. Alternatively (or additionally), self-injury may be a response to factors within the environment itself.

We discussed in *Chapter 5* how self-injury may serve important functions in relation to the institution, and listed some possible questions to consider about the role of the institution and its staff and users in giving rise to self-injury. Where self-injury is particularly prevalent, or seems to happen in 'rashes', it is important to try to understand what is going on. Staff need to talk with clients, individually and as a group, to find out what they see as the reasons for the self-injury. Given the opportunity to be heard sympathetically and taken seriously, many residents will be prepared to voice problems and address issues for the group, and to be creative in finding solutions.

Ways of addressing the problem of apparent 'rashes' or 'contagion' include:

- ensuring that all residents have the attention and support they need;
- treating all individuals with respect, as people with rights, views, abilities and strengths;
- encouraging direct verbal expression of feelings, conflicts and difficulties;
- fostering a culture of mutual support and co-operation, both within the client group and between residents and staff;
- giving residents as much say as possible in their own lives and in the circumstances and running of their present environment;
- providing safe channels through which grievances can be reported and properly followed up;
- ensuring that residents have access to sufficient stimulating, purposeful activities and opportunities for social contact (boredom and isolation can foster self-injury, and evenings may be a particular problem);
- providing opportunities for individuals to safely discharge anger, tension and frustration, for example, a punchbag, various sports;
- ensuring that there are effective means for conflict between staff to be resolved (Aldridge, 1988).

The impact of self-injury on staff

Staff in residential and in-patient settings report that self-injury can make enormous demands on staff time and can interfere with their ability to run the unit smoothly and to meet the needs of all clients. Where staff feel persistently overburdened, they may become angry and punitive towards a resident who frequently self-injures or threatens to do so, and seems 'too demanding'. The emotional impact of self-injury may also be particularly strong for those working in residential and in-patient settings. Staff may experience considerable distress and strain through witnessing repeated incidents of self-injury, attempting to anticipate and control risk, and so on. Staff on units where people who self-injure are not subject to close control report sometimes feeling dread and horror of what they may find on opening a bedroom or bathroom door. (Fortunately, the *fear* of what might happen is usually far worse than the *reality* of witnessing any injuries which are inflicted.)

The demands placed on staff by self-injury tend to arise from the following.

Measures taken to prevent self-injury. Measures such as close observation are extremely costly in staff time. It was seen in *Chapter 5* that clients (and staff) may benefit from an approach which does not rely on control of self-injury by staff.

The support needs of individuals who self-injure. Staffing levels may need to be increased. It is particularly important to maintain adequate staffing levels during times of the day when self-injury seems to increase – usually in the evening. However, with the best will in the world staff cannot be available at every moment for every person. Residents may be able to share more support with each other, and ways of promoting this (perhaps through more group-work, or 'buddying' schemes) could be explored. Individuals can also be helped to develop ways of coping and expressing themselves which do not require the immediate involvement of staff.

Dealing with injuries. In residential and inpatient settings there may be repeated instances of self-injury, perhaps on the part of several clients at any one time. This can lead to staff spending a lot of time reactively dealing with injuries.

It can be helpful for people who self-injure to take as much responsibility as they can cope with for dealing with their own injuries. Often injuries are minor, and people can care adequately for them if they are provided with a first aid kit and some simple instruction. (They may still need some emotional support and should not simply be abandoned or ignored.) It is a good idea for staff in agencies without medical facilities to try to foster relationships with GPs and A and E staff, who will then be more prepared to respond supportively to residents needing treatment for more severe injuries.

The Particular Issues Arising in Hospital In-Patient Settings

In-patient psychiatric units are likely to be a main source of any intensive treatment available for most people who self-injure. They are able to provide a level of support which is rarely available in any other setting. Many people who self-injure say that they at times feel the need of 'asylum', that is, for a place where they can go for a while to feel safe, to receive some care and help and to take some respite from the pressures of their lives outside (Arnold, 1995). However, while someone may benefit from the support, protection and treatment offered by a psychiatric hospital, often aspects of psychiatric in-patient treatment are not beneficial in the long-term to someone struggling with the problems of self-injury.

The nature of a psychiatric in-patient setting raises a range of important issues and dilemmas. The common expectation that staff will prevent self-injury is one element of a general culture or expectation that in-patient settings take care of patients in something of a parental fashion. The treatment of psychological distress in a medical setting implies that such distress, like a physical symptom, stems from illness which can be made better by medical and nursing staff. The role of the patient within the medical model is inherently passive: it is to follow the prescribed treatment of an 'expert' who has diagnosed what is wrong with them. In this context patients are likely to hand over a large measure of responsibility to the hospital and its staff. Emotional distress and associated behaviour may be seen as something staff should control and cure. This transfer of responsibility (and with it power) for the self can be dangerous medically, and a bad thing psychologically, since the individual is effectively encouraged to abdicate responsibility for their own safety and for their own life, feelings and actions.

Where there is an expectation that self-injury will be prevented and mental distress 'cured' (coupled with considerable power to impose treatments), there often results an over-emphasis on the use of medication, together with the application of measures such as compulsory admission, close observation and supervision of patients or stringent behaviour modification programmes. As we discussed in *Chapter 5*, this can result in problems of disempowerment and the reinforcement of ideas which underpin self-injury (that is, that emotional distress is dealt with by immediate physical solutions, or that the person is bad and out of control).

Someone coming into a psychiatric hospital as an in-patient (especially for the first time) may experience a range of very powerful emotions. Clearly, they are likely to be extremely distressed already, hence the decision to admit them. They are away from the familiarity, roles, supports and relationships of their home, community and normal daily life. Although they may feel relieved that their distress is being recognized and that they are to receive help, they may also, however, feel terrified of the fact of being in a 'mental hospital', by the behaviour and distress of other patients, and possibly by locked doors and windows. They may feel powerless and afraid of what is to be done to them, especially if their admission was not planned. (The situation of some patients, especially, but not exclusively, women, is made even more traumatic by being subjected to sexual harassment or assault from other patients or staff.)

In the strange environment of hospital, most patients are likely to try to ease their discomfort by observing and adopting ways in which other patients behave. Much of this will be encouraged by, and helpful to, staff; for example fitting in with routines of mealtimes, drug rounds, occupational therapy, ward rounds, and so on. Patients are expected to comply with unspoken norms of behaviour, which may include things which are very different from normal adult behaviour outside hospital, such as being passive and obedient, and accepting restrictions on freedom. Amongst less approved 'norms' of behaviour which patients may also adopt may be self-injury. Clearly this is 'copying', but the reasons for it are not as simple as the word may imply.

It may also appear that self-injury is a major means by which distress is signalled in the hospital environment. If new patients are not told clearly that support is available for their distress, and encouraged to draw on this, they may not feel confident about approaching staff directly to voice their feelings. Instead, they may use indirect means of communication which they observe as being effective, including self-injury.

Whilst in their usual home environment, individuals may feel able to make use of means of expressing feelings (such as crying, having rows, or slamming doors) which are not condoned in hospital. It is not unusual for users of psychiatric services to say that they feel very constrained in expressing strong feelings, which are often seen as warranting control with medication, rather than being heard and accepted.

'If you get angry they give you drugs. If you cry, they tell you to come and socialize or do OT. If you laugh, they say you're hysterical and you've got to calm down. It makes you crazy.'

An alternative model

We have argued that some elements of the culture and ways of managing self-injury in hospital settings may be counter-productive. Patients may appear to 'improve' for a while as their behaviour is controlled, but little real change may take place, so that they repeatedly return to hospital over many years. There is considerable scope, however, for in-patient services to provide beneficial treatment to individuals who self-injure. As we discussed in *Chapter 5*, approaches which help the patient to express and manage their own feelings and exercise more choice about their own behaviour will result in learning which they will be able to use in supporting themselves outside hospital. Responses which convey respect and understanding will have a positive effect on self-esteem and self-understanding.

An example of such an alternative approach is that recently introduced in a unit at the Bethlem Royal Hospital for people who self-injure severely (Jane Bunclark, 1996, conference paper and personal communication.) Here the former approach emphasized the prevention of self-injury by traditional and sometimes intrusive or coercive means. This approach was abandoned following recognition that it resulted in many problems: staff and patients were forced into a power struggle; any self-injury, however minor, was experienced by staff as a 'failure' on their part; and patients prevented from injuring themselves simply replaced this behaviour with other forms of 'self-harm', such as starving themselves or refusing to drink. The new approach involves allowing patients to exercise choice and control over their own self-injury. Patients are helped to identify and cope with feelings and experiences which seem to act as triggers to their self-injury. They work with staff on 'safety planning', which involves anticipating and planning ways of dealing with crises which might precipitate self-injury. Patients are encouraged to build their own understanding of their self-injury and to develop alternative means of expression and coping. Staff report that in general this approach has worked well and feel that the environment has become far more 'therapeutic', in that the real causes of distress and self-injury are being tackled, rather than the emphasis remaining on short-term symptom control. Where at times this approach has proved insufficient to prevent severe self-injury, staff and patients have negotiated an agreement whereby staff (with the patient's prior permission) may intervene should self-injury reach a certain level. Whilst this involves, at the time, the problematic element of coercion, the patient has at least previously taken a full part in the decision to limit their self-injury in this way.

To ask hospital staff who are charged with patients' safety and well-being to take a less interventionist approach and to hand back responsibility for self-injury to patients themselves places a new type of stress upon them. Supportive guidelines and back-up from management as well as ongoing supervision and support are needed to enable staff to work in such a way.

We have discussed how patients who self-injure may benefit from a more empowering approach to their situation. More broadly, we would suggest that it would be helpful for psychiatric units to base their approach on a model which viewed self-injury as an aspect of the effects of trauma. Within this model, people are treated as capable adults who simply need to deal with something which has happened to them. The emphasis is on taking control of one's own recovery from 'injury'. Elements of a therapeutic milieu which would help someone in respect of self-injury include safety, support, containment, and the principle that feelings are okay and can be tolerated.

The Particular Issues Arising in Prisons and Secure Settings

Prisons, special hospitals and secure units are the settings in which some of the highest incidences of self-injury are found, amongst both men and women (Winchel and Stanley, 1991). Young people in prison seem to be particularly likely to self-injure. There are a number of reasons for the high levels of self-injury seen in secure environments.

The very nature of imprisonment is itself likely to contribute to the high incidence of self-injury. A number of studies in secure environments have identified factors such as environmental restriction, boredom and under-occupation as significant in self-injury (see, for example, Holloway Project Committee, 1985). Confinement under the control of others brings feelings of powerlessness and frustration, which may trigger self-injury (Cookson, 1977). Paradoxically, an inmate who is viewed as likely to self-injure will often be subjected to even higher levels of supervision and control, which in turn may add to the frustrations and isolation which make self-injury more likely. In his study of self-injury within a British special hospital, Burrow (1992) found that women patients in particular were subjected to a variety of powerful measures (often in combination) designed to prevent what was often quite minor self-injury, including close observation, seclusion, medication and the use of restraint garments. Burrow noted that such measures were sometimes applied *following* acts of self-injury, when the crisis which had triggered the individual's self-injury had abated, so that 'prevention' was in any event no longer relevant. There is evidence that self-mutilation is particularly likely to occur during periods of solitary confinement (Cullen, 1985). Paradoxically this supposedly 'preventative' measure is still often applied to inmates who injure themselves, despite the recommendation of a Home Office study (HMSO, 1990) that isolation was not suitable for suicidal inmates and that 'interactive supervision' should be used, rather than 'passive observation' of those considered at risk of harming themselves.

The lack of direct control over their own life and circumstances may result in an inmate attempting to exert some influence through self-injury, perhaps as a means of inducing the prison authorities to move them to a different part of the prison. The situation of those on remand or facing court appearances is particularly stressful, with fear and uncertainty making self-injury (as well as suicide attempts) more likely. Where inmates are facing long sentences (or even, as in special hospitals, having no release date) they may feel depressed and demoralized, with little motivation to deal positively with their situation or feelings, so that self-injury may be perpetuated.

In prisons and secure hospitals there is usually a lack of privacy and of physical space in which to move around. (It is significant in this respect to note that self-destructive behaviour, such as self-biting, is also found amongst animals who are imprisoned in cages. The prison environment is often noisy and chaotic, with inmates (particularly in hospital settings) frequently witnessing others' expressions of distress. Inmates are separated from their families and friends and may feel they receive little support or caring.

Although staff may offer emotional support where possible, the scope for doing so is limited by both the high inmate to staff ratios, and by the nature of the disciplinary role to which staff have to give priority. (In a study of young female inmates, Cullen (1985) found that many perceived their environment as unsupportive and felt over-controlled by staff.) Conflict amongst prisoners (and staff) is likely to be particularly distressing in a context where people are confined together in close proximity. This may contribute to feelings of anxiety and lack of safety which drive an inmate to self-injure.

People in secure environments are removed from the goals, structure and responsibilities of their normal lives, which may usually provide them with some motivation and stability. They may experience enormous grief, dislocation and homesickness. Separation from children may be particularly devastating, especially for a woman who does not have a partner who will keep the home and childcare going, with the result that her children go into care. This and/or her length of sentence may mean a woman effectively loses her children. For both men and women in prison, marriages and important relationships outside may suffer or break down. News of problems such as these can often trigger self-injury, and inmates need support to cope with such difficulties when they are able to do little to improve the outside situation.

Inmates may be under-occupied and lack social and sensory stimulation (this is especially likely to be the case amongst those 'vulnerable prisoners' who spend a lot of time alone in their cells). Inmate members of a support group in a women's prison hospital wing reported to us that they 'had too much time to think'. Some had been stopped from attending daily work and craft activities because of staff's concern that these would provide them with access to objects which they could use to harm themselves. Where they had little else to do, any feelings of anxiety or distress were likely to escalate to the point of desperation. People in prison are denied many of their normal emotional outlets (Bach-Y-Rita, 1974), and there may be few sanctioned ways of expressing and receiving acknowledgement for feelings of distress, anger and so on. In such a context self-injury may present itself as the only means to vent feelings which seem unbearable.

There are aspects of life within a prison or secure hospital which may be highly reminiscent to individuals of abuse they suffered as a child. Confinement and powerlessness themselves may evoke feelings of terror and victimization. Trauma may be restimulated by the use of control and restraint methods; strip-searching; being watched by staff looking through observation-holes or coming into cells without warning; emotional and sexual harassment and abuse by staff (Potier, 1993), and bullying and abuse (including sexual assault) by other prisoners. These things would be distressing in themselves to anyone, but to someone who was abused as a child (a common background amongst inmates) they may be especially traumatic. Prisoners may try to cope with this trauma by adopting or increasing self-injury.

In some cases, self-injury may be adopted by a prisoner wishing to become part of a prison subculture, whose norms and modes of expression include self-injury. Wounds and scars may be a means of obtaining status or credibility and prisoners may be subject to peer pressure to harm themselves. Self-injury may also be a means of protest and rebellion against the prison authorities and staff. However, it is not always the case that self-injury is approved by the subculture of secure settings. In interviewing prison staff and inmates we have also been told of the stigmatization and contempt which prisoners may show towards those who self-injure. In any event, it is very important that self-injury amongst inmates should not simply be dismissed as 'normal' or 'copying', since it often stems from an individual's real distress.

Responding to the problem of self-injury in secure environments

The scale of self-injury in secure settings and the danger and distress which this causes to inmates and patients (as well as to staff) clearly need to be addressed. Some of the factors which make self-injury so prevalent in secure settings are intrinsic and there may be little scope for change. For example, confinement is the *sine qua non* of the prisoner's situation. However, certain aspects of this which exacerbate the situation may be open to changes which would help reduce distress and self-injury. Such (in our view) desirable changes include:

- reductions in overcrowding; greater privacy;
- improvements in physical conditions and food;
- more time spent out of cells and involved in work, education, exercise, social and other meaningful activities;

- placing young people in institutions appropriate to their age and needs, rather than in adult prisons/units;
- better staff to inmate ratios (perhaps with staff having responsibility for smaller groups of inmates);
- the acknowledgement and prevention of assault, sexual harassment and bullying;
- more contact with (and proximity to) families and friends outside;
- better channels for communication and expression/resolution of grievances;
- an emphasis by staff on listening to and supporting, rather than simply controlling, inmates who self-injure. This underlines the need for appropriate training for staff charged with the control and care of distressed inmates.

Most of these measures would require political will and the allocation of substantially increased resources. However, if a solution to levels of self-injury (and similarly, suicide) is to be found, these issues need to be addressed.

A range of other measures may be helpful in tackling self-injury in secure settings. Cullen (1985) found the lowest rate of self-injury amongst female offenders within a unit which had instituted a 'therapeutic regime', where 'support, expression, involvement and personal problem-orientation' were rated as of primary importance. Some elements of such a therapeutic regime helpful for inmates/patients who self-injure would include the following:

- an atmosphere of support for the expression of feelings and problems;
- the opportunity to talk out feelings before the individual becomes so 'wound up' that self-injury feels like the only option. Inmates would need to be able to tell staff they feel distressed without having to fear that they will immediately be subjected to measures to control self-injury, such as searching, or placement in 'strip cells';
- means of safely expressing anger, such as in a 'soft' room where inmates could hit walls, or a punchbag;
- groupwork, allowing the discussion of difficulties and of ways to cope. Members of support/therapy groups for women who self-injure at Ashworth Special Hospital and Holloway Prison reported that they found groupwork helpful in raising their self-esteem, providing opportunities for sharing feelings, experiences and ideas, developing their understanding of their behaviour, and learning something valuable to use in their lives, including means of coping without self-injury (Liebling, Chipchase and Velangi, 1996; Kelland, 1995);

- schemes involving individual inmates as 'therapeutic agents' (or 'buddies'), supporting and sharing responsibility for each other (Gardner and Cowdrey, 1985);
- work aimed at raising self-esteem;
- the opportunity for ongoing, regular and consistent counselling/ therapy with a worker not involved in a disciplinary role;
- involvement in decision-making and the day-to-day running of the unit (Offer and Barglow, 1960). A generally collaborative problem- and conflict-solving orientation.

Summary

In this chapter we have discussed some of the challenges and possibilities for working with people who self-injure in a range of community and institutional/residential settings. Whilst the settings in which such people are encountered vary in their nature and roles, it is clear in each case that there is considerable scope for helpful and effective responses to those who injure themselves. Key principles in each case include understanding of the distress reflected in self-injury, and willingness to recognize where the institution itself may be contributing to this distress. In responding to individuals who injure themselves, approaches emphasizing sensitivity, support and empowerment can be employed in all settings.

7. Therapy with People who Self-Injure

In this chapter we will give some thought to the therapy situation. We will aim to highlight the issues surrounding self-mutilation as they appear in the therapeutic setting, and offer first ideas and then practical suggestions which can be incorporated by therapists into their own approaches.

We emphasize very strongly that we do not aim in this chapter to teach therapy to those who have no specialist skills in this particular area of work. The chapter is aimed at therapists of various backgrounds and therapeutic persuasions who are *already* working in various capacities with difficult problems and deep levels of distress in their patients. Individuals who are not psychotherapists as such, but who may be working with self-injury in various other ways, are advised to refer to *Chapters 5* and *6*.

Similarly, not all patients who self-mutilate may be suited to psychotherapy, nor want to work in this manner. Nevertheless, individuals who self-injure are eloquent about the central importance in their lives of the reactions and approach to them by others. Referring the reader once again to *Chapters 5* and *6*, it is clear that there are many therapeutic benefits for all such individuals in empathic, validating environments that exist outside of the context of formal therapy sessions.

Our starting point for therapy is that self-mutilation is instrumental: it serves important psychological functions. Self-mutilation is employed as a means of coping with intolerable levels of anxiety, of self-soothing and distraction from pain, and of recovery from periods of dissociation or absence from the self. As we have already seen, via these functions, self-mutilation is highly efficient at relieving distress and therefore intensely reinforcing. For this reason, it may be extremely difficult for people to give up.

In addition, we have seen that self-mutilation may also represent a complicated act of destruction. The person who injures their body in this instance is carrying out an act which contains the two basic elements of a need to destroy on the one hand, and a need for victimization on the other. During the act of self-mutilation this person is both the abuser or punisher of the body; and at the same time the victim and receiver of punishment. The patient's awareness of one aspect may be stronger than their awareness of the other.

This is further complicated by the fact that the 'abuser' element may be highly ambivalent and full of remorse. Similarly the element that is hurt can be experienced as either the innocent frightened victim, or the 'bad' person who is deserving of the punishment; or contain aspects of both.

Therapist Issues

Self-mutilation can be frightening for either the therapist or the patient, or both. In order to avoid panic and horror, and ensure a safe therapeutic space, it is of paramount importance therefore that the therapist have a commitment to understanding the meaning of this behaviour, and her own responses to it. This understanding, and the therapeutic relationship which contains it, are the constituents of the therapy which avoids making the cessation of self-mutilation its goal.

In working with self-mutilation, as elsewhere in abuse work, perhaps the most fundamental aspect of working with integrity for the therapist is to gain awareness of, and to deal satisfactorily with, one's own uncomfortable reactions and feelings. The therapist can monitor such feelings on a regular basis when writing up session notes and later in supervision. Common headings for these may include: *Shock, horror and disgust; Incomprehension; Fear and anxiety; Distress and sadness; Anger and frustration; Powerlessness and inadequacy.* The objective of such monitoring is to remain aware of the therapist's own progress in dealing with these difficult feelings as the patient progresses through their own work.

It is natural and understandable that people working with individuals who self-injure will struggle with such difficult feelings and reactions. The paramount question then becomes how to work effectively in this context. The answer to this rests almost solely on the necessity for therapists to have access to appropriate supervision and support, and, possibly, personal therapy. Once again, it is assumed that therapists who are reading this chapter and working with individuals who self-injure severely will already have an effective grasp of abuse work.

A Philosophical Position

This section is concerned with the general orientation that we think it important for the therapist to bring to this work. The therapist's psychological knowledge and insight into her own feelings are paramount. In addition, we consider that in working with self-mutilation, the prejudices, beliefs, and idealistic opinions of the therapist influence the outcome more strongly than the techniques applied. In the therapeutic situation, the philosophical position may be defined in the form of key statements.

Self-mutilation is not an 'illness'

The therapist and the patient eschew a pathological view of the behaviour. Self-mutilation is not a disorder, nor even a symptom of disorder. To the extent that therapy focuses on self-mutilation at all, the major work converges on the functional, adaptive, and instrumental nature of this behaviour. Both therapist and patient realize that even the most violent forms of self-mutilation contain an element of self-preservation, and exist for the purpose of defining, understanding and managing deep emotional pain.

The therapy does not aim at treatment for self-mutilation *per se*. There is undoubtedly a connection between therapy and self-mutilation and people who are in treatment may stop self mutilating. That is usually because the therapy is aimed at the underlying pain and when the therapy undertakes this, the need for self-mutilation decreases. Sometimes, and for the same reason, awareness of the underlying pain and feelings which are elicited in therapy can cause a transient increase in the need to self-injure or an aggravation in the nature of the self-mutilation. The therapist does not see this as a sign that the patient is 'worsening' but rather that she is bringing into awareness previously inaccessible or unbearable feelings. The fact that the therapist does not see increases in self-mutilation as a failure removes some of the shame that may be involved for the patient, who may then be able to continue to move closer to more and more of this upsetting material. The therapist's awareness of escalations in the severity of self-injury should alert her to the need to adjust the pacing and focus of the work appropriately, so that the patient is not overwhelmed and retraumatized, but is helped to develop her own internal and external support systems so that she can tolerate the feelings which the work evokes.

The therapist does not intervene in the self-mutilation

The therapist does not insist, require, or ask that the patient stop the self-mutilating behaviour. But this does not mean that the therapist minimizes or colludes with the mutilation. The therapist attempts to understand the behaviour and seeks to promote her patient's understanding of it as an obstacle to self-integration. Whilst acknowledging the self-preserving functions which self-mutilation has served, she also seeks, when appropriate, to help her patient understand the self-loathing and self-destructive aspects of the behaviour, and to explore alternative means by which the individual may cope and express themselves.

The therapist is concerned, and may show her concern about the injury itself. Nevertheless, the main concern is for the pain, fear or shame that the patient is experiencing, or was experiencing, at the time of the mutilation.

The therapist need not monitor the self-injury nor make regular enquiries as to the frequency or extent of the behaviour. This does not mean that self-mutilation should not be talked about; in fact, it is important to communicate that it is something which can be raised, explored and understood together, and that the person will not be 'told off' or shamed because of it. It is likely that the patient will fear exposing her self-mutilation, in the same way that she fears exposing the pain which it reflects. The therapist who makes enquiries into areas such as self-mutilation should ensure that this does not come across as a violation or an intrusion into private matters. The therapist avoids emotionally charged phraseology and prefers a matter of fact way of speaking which describes events clearly.

The therapist is able to discuss self-mutilation

Although we do not advocate asking about details at length, it is important for the therapist to be able to hear and to 'hold'; that is, to contain safely her own and her patient's awareness of the details of the self-injurious activities revealed by the patient. The foundation of the therapist's work is 'being there' for the patient. She contains her need to 'do something' in favour of her patient's need to be held.

Often, therapeutic work on the issues underlying self-mutilation will be accompanied by a falling away of self-mutilation as the individual becomes more able to deal with and integrate her experiences. However, this may take considerable time, and in the meantime, the therapist should be open and alert to disclosure of fluctuations in the frequency and severity of self-mutilation.

In this area of work, it is important for the therapist to be able to discuss 'the body' in a more general sense. For most therapists, this involves additional work, as few are comfortable discussing such matters as body functioning and physical health, sex and sexual practices, and so on. This does not mean that the therapist should impose an interest in the physical aspects of her patient's problem on herself or her patient. The issue is more one of creating an environment for both therapist and patient where the importance of the meaning of the body in understanding distress can be processed.

The drawback of asking questions about self-mutilation to a person just beginning in therapy is that they may experience these as assumptions made by the therapist, and feel stigmatized by these assumptions. This is all the more likely if particular aspects of a patient's history (for example, sexual abuse in childhood) are leading the therapist's questions into the area of self-inflicted harm. A more appropriate framework for introducing the possibility of self-mutilation might be in the context of discussions about issues of emotional and physical safety.

The advantages of asking questions that encourage patients to reveal their self-mutilating behaviour are mainly that contrary to the prevalent view that self-mutilation is an attention-seeking behaviour, most women who hurt themselves do so in secret, and attempt to hide the problem. The therapist, by creating an environment where this behaviour can be acknowledged, named, and perhaps even seen to be not uncommon, is in fact providing acceptance and what may well be the first step towards a therapeutic relationship.

Disclosure of self-mutilation need not mean that the patient is prepared to talk at length about this aspect of their life. Even if revealed spontaneously it should not be assumed that the self-mutilation should become the focus of the therapist's attention.

The therapist and patient may also need to discuss the place that self-mutilation has in their relationship, and the extent to which it may carry 'messages' about this, as well as about past experiences in the patient's life. Sometimes self-mutilation can reflect tensions, hostility, or longings in the therapeutic relationship. However we would warn against the therapist assuming every time the patient discloses an incident of self-injury that this relates to the therapy.

Self-mutilation has a meaning

Several assumptions which we have elaborated on earlier in this book comprise the theoretical position. An application of this position to the therapy situation has one main focus: the work of the therapy centres on what lies beneath the self-mutilation. In *Chapter 4* we organized the many meanings and functions of self-mutilation under five main themes:

1. themes of 'self' and increasing autonomy and control;
2. the many functions to do with 'coping';
3. the self-destructive aspects of 'sacrifice' and 'getting rid of';
4. re-enactment and the demonstration to oneself of one's experience; and finally,
5. 'interpersonal' functions to do with the meaning and process of relationships.

The last two themes, combining as they do the demonstration to oneself and to others of the pain and distress underlying self-mutilation, can be said to combine into a theme we might think of as 'validation'.

Since in our view self-mutilation is not itself a 'disorder', but a reflection of, and means of coping with, painful experiences and difficulties, it follows that the focus and bulk of the work in therapy concerns these underlying experiences and difficulties.

A Theoretical Position

In the following section we will revisit in critical detail some of the issues that arise from theoretical perspectives of self-injury in the therapeutic setting. What is important in every case is that the therapist is careful not to oversimplify her understanding of self-mutilation. Even more importantly, she is careful to not impose her understanding of the function of the behaviour on her patient.

Links with past and present

There exists a strong link between self-mutilating behaviour and a person's history of maltreatment, loss and abandonment. What the therapy consists of essentially is making this link explicit. However, self-mutilation can occur in the absence of immediate awareness of any difficulties in the past, and the individual may construe it as a fresh coping mechanism in response to their current situation. Indeed, it may well be the case that a patient's current life circumstances themselves are extremely difficult. Therapy should pay attention to the function of the self-mutilating behaviour in the present setting, as well as in relation to past experience. This also makes it possible to think about why the current situation exceeds the person's capacity to cope in their regular ways.

An important aspect of therapy in this respect is the facilitating of an understanding of sexual experiences and fantasies as they relate to self-mutilation. The sexual material itself presents the therapist with many of the difficulties we mentioned in relation to self-mutilation. It is important that in a discussion of sex or sexual practices the therapist be self-aware, in order to deal with their reactions and to communicate clearly and safely.

Social issues

We outlined in *Chapter 3* the importance of the therapist having an awareness of social issues as they impact on the individual's self-mutilating. Experiences such as the ones we have discussed, and in particular maltreatment, are inextricably linked to political issues. The elements that underlie self-mutilation occur within a socio-cultural context of power inequality. Directly or indirectly the therapy links an individual's experiences and feelings about powerlessness to their reflecting on inequalities of a wider nature within the family, the system, and eventually society as a whole. In *Chapter 3* we offered some of the ways in which these links can be made. Working in a political way may be difficult for individual practitioners, particularly in institutional settings. Practitioners who do attempt to expose and challenge the status quo may soon find themselves being undermined, marginalized or punished. Believing and supporting patients whose problems carry strong connotations of political or social issues may leave therapists feeling anxious and vulnerable. However, we consider, with other therapists who work in this manner (Herman, 1992) , that the rewards to ourselves and to our patients manifest themselves in achieving a more meaningful form of integration. We consider that in order to face the unspeakable distress that leads our patients to self-injure horribly, we and they must draw on our thoughtfulness, maturity and integrity in the most comprehensive sense.

Communicating feelings

There is frequently a link between self-mutilating behaviour and difficulties with experiencing and verbalizing strong emotional material. The communicative significance of self-injury has been studied quite convincingly, particularly in persons with developmental disabilities (Carr and Durand, 1985). It is thought that individuals with limited repertoires for expression, or who are in an environment which does not support or facilitate effective communication, have learned alternative, functionally-equivalent means of self-expression. Even though they appear maladaptive, these may serve the same purpose effectively. Thus in certain situations, self-mutilation may serve the same function as using language.

The therapy helps provide mastery over strong emotions by facilitating their communication and eventually putting them into words. The ability to speak about what happened to one, and how it made one feel is linked directly to the acquiring of control over the effects of trauma and eventually towards integration.

It becomes more possible to give up self-mutilation when traumatic feelings become understood and accepted as part of the self, and not a separate entity which exists oppressively outside the ability of the self to understand and put experiences into words. Bessel van der Kolk *et al.* (1996) have described experimental evidence of what may be involved in this process physically and psychologically. Perhaps paradoxically, it appears furthermore as though once the full agony has become understood to the individual as 'This is how I feel', 'This happened to me' , or 'This is part of myself', it becomes harder to self-injure. There is less need to do so perhaps, as more potent means of communication are adopted; but there is also a deepening of respect for oneself which comes with greater understanding, and, with it, less willingness to hurt oneself. The role of the therapist in relation to this aspect of the work is to encourage and facilitate the patient in expressing their feelings and experiences in new ways. This may take considerable time and creativity and therapists may find that means of expression such as drawing, photography, or writing, are very helpful for people who find it hard to verbalize their experience.

Pain, anxiety and addiction

Within self-mutilation, physical pain may serve a function of its own. It may be useful for the therapy to explore separately the functions of the self-injurious act as one issue, and the functions of its physical consequences, such as pain, as another.

As we have seen in *Chapter 4*, one biological model (van der Kolk, 1988) suggests that self-mutilation may induce analgesia through the release of endogenous opioids and concurrently an altered state of consciousness. This has led to suggestions that people who self-mutilate may have an 'addiction' to what has become a powerful reinforcer. The phenomenon of negative reinforcement (making something aversive, such as anxiety, stop) is well understood, and we concur that to elaborate this in therapy could be very useful. The danger in formulating this as an addiction, with all the negative connotations that this implies, is to pathologize the process unnecessarily. This can in turn lead to a dangerously simplistic approach aimed solely at symptom removal. It is beneficial, however, to discuss the 'addictive' *quality* of self-injury in the context of normal human response, and how the ability to make aversive experience retreat can become highly reinforcing.

The therapist introduces the notion that anxiety and distressing feelings do not have to be made to 'go away' at all cost, but that it is possible to gradually face elements that were once felt to be intolerable and to bear them. The patient and therapist should also explore means of managing and coping with distress that feels intolerable so that self-mutilation is not the only means at the person's disposal.

Re-enactment

Some clinicians and authors have stressed the view that self-mutilation constitutes a re-enactment of maltreatment events that closely approximates the details of the experience. In our opinion, it is the *feelings* engendered by childhood maltreatment, rather than the events themselves which have the stronger link with adult self-mutilation. Dusty Miller (1994) proposes 'Trauma Re-enactment Syndrome' to describe the cycle of negative feelings and beliefs that lead to self-mutilation, which in turn engenders guilt and further negative feeling. McCann and Pearlman (1990) frame the idea of re-enactment in the broader context of self-destructive behaviours as trauma responses. They talk about the re-enactment aspect of these behaviours as being very subtle and occurring without the patient's conscious awareness of their meaning. The implication is that once the symbolic purpose of these re-enactments through self-mutilation has been discovered and interpreted, the behaviour decreases. With regard to self-mutilation, our view is that, while very useful, interpretation alone is unlikely to be sufficient in most cases, where self-mutilation has become central to the individual's life and coping. In understanding the meaning of self-mutilation the therapy needs to go beyond the symbolic re-enactment aspects of the self-mutilation and address their functional and social purpose as a means of addressing the difficulty of giving them up, even after they have been interpreted.

Rescue fantasies

Some clinical authors such as Gil (1988) and Courtois (1988) have mentioned that the purpose of self-mutilation may be to reflect a deep wish to be rescued by the therapist. We agree that it is important to address the likelihood that this may exist, and the powerful nature of the meaning of this to the relationship. It is essential however not to overlook the *therapist's* urgent need to rescue, which somewhat precludes the patient having responsibility for bringing this behaviour under control. The therapist should always seek to facilitate the development of the patient's control and power within their own life. Whilst the therapist is flexible and offers caring and support, she does not encourage over-dependency in relation to the self-mutilation through, for example setting up a 'rescuing' procedure of excessive telephone calls and emergency sessions. She encourages the patient to cope, putting her in charge of her own recovery. The therapist emphasizes at every appropriate stage the patient's own value systems and their need to be in control of their own life.

Validation

It is essential in this therapeutic work to be supportive towards and validating of the patient, and to underline the adaptive purpose of their distressing behaviours. Holmes (1995) in arguing the importance of support within formal psychotherapies writes, 'Most supportive techniques have at their base the assignment of positive meaning to what appear to be negative situations'. Positive meanings appear sometimes to be interpreted as 'reframing'. This usually implies that the therapist considers a behaviour to be maladaptive but looks nevertheless for a 'silver lining' aspect to the behaviour in order to mitigate the experience of failure. Rockland (1987) describes just such an approach in treating self-mutilation where he presents in the first instance a therapeutic stance based on his 'severe disapproval' and behavioural strategies to manage self-mutilation. If this therapeutic stance fails, *then* Rockland says the therapist needs to 'remind herself that the patient is doing the very best she can' and suggests a supportive approach based on putting to one side concerns about self-mutilation in favour of 'improving the rest of the patient's life'.

In our opinion, there is a huge difference between Rockland's and other 'reframing and paradox' approaches, and validation in therapy of the kind we advocate. The difference is in the quality of the message which comes from the therapist. What is needed to convey this with integrity is an *internal acceptance* and respect on the part of the therapist for the patient's 'solution' to their difficulties.

Linehan (1993) has developed an approach to therapy with 'borderline' patients who self-harm, which she calls *Dialectic Behaviour Therapy*. Validation of the patient's experience and avoiding blaming the patient underlie Linehan's framework significantly. However, she points out that in therapy this can pose a significant challenge: to validate the patient's current capabilities and behaviours (and presumably ideas and emotions) and at the same time focus on skills training and behaviour change. To accomplish this, Linehan combines conventional behavioural and cognitive strategies aimed at change, with strategies derived from the Zen Buddhist concept of 'mindfulness'. Much of this is very interesting conceptually, and empirical evidence for the effectiveness of this integrated approach (Linehan, 1993) is beginning to accumulate. We are, as we have said before, opposed, however, to Linehan's apparent assumption that it is a necessary starting point for therapy for the patient to be told that her self-mutilating is 'unacceptable'. Far from being validating, this form of authoritarian control seems at odds with Linehan's own approach in fact, particularly her advocacy of not blaming the victim. Linehan herself reports that blame is difficult to avoid; the reasons therefore, why the *therapist* may find her patient's self-mutilation 'unacceptable' certainly need to be validated and processed, as we have described. However, we can see no advantage in being negatively judgemental and unsupportive. We consider that the therapist needs always to be aware of the danger of undermining the patient's autonomy and responsibility.

A Framework for the Therapy

The following section aims to present the elements of a therapeutic framework which can be used by any therapist working with patients who self-mutilate. Therapists who are grounded in particular schools of thinking may find that they need to adapt or adjust some of their methods to meet the needs of the framework described in this chapter. However, self-mutilation provides only one example of a therapy where this may be necessary. It is becoming widely recognized that psychosocial problems of this depth and complexity require less technically rigid, more integrated approaches. This therapy aims to create an environment where the focus is on thoughts, feelings, memories and problems; in other words, primarily on conscious life and awareness, rather than on a pursuit of 'The Unconscious'. The relationship with the therapist is very important, particularly those aspects of the therapist's behaviour which demonstrate that she is comfortable with self-mutilation and other forms of 'badness' and that she can tolerate hostility. However, the therapist does not address self-injury primarily in terms of 'transference interpretations', or suggestions that this behaviour is directed primarily at the therapist, as these are not particularly helpful in this type of work (Babiker, 1995). There is an open relationship between the therapist and the patient, with the therapist taking part in discussing goals for therapy, contributing her views in active and open ways and fostering the patient's adaptive defences. She encourages the patient to cope, putting her in charge of her own recovery, and fostering security and continuity in the relationship. The therapist answers questions appropriately and honestly, offers feedback; and re-orients towards reality when necessary.

When the therapist knows that the particular history of her patient has made her very frightened by and mistrustful of intimate relationships, the therapist may need to maintain an appropriate distance. Even then, the therapist fosters security and consistency and works to create a 'safe' environment where intimacy is facilitated, and is helpful and positive, even when the results of this are likely to take a long time. The therapist emphasizes at every appropriate stage the patient's own value systems and their need to be in control of their own life.

Making a relationship

Regardless of the type of therapy being undertaken, the first step in making a relationship is always to create a safe environment. Without this, the therapy should not proceed. Safety means that the patient's need for acceptance on their terms is possible. It means also

137

that the therapist is willing and able to undertake the work. Safety may mean that environmental factors in the patient's life have to take precedence for a while, and the therapist has to engage in working with her patient to establish that her living situation in all its aspects, is safe. She endeavours to make sure her patient has a plan for self-protection in danger and in crises, including if acceptable, a plan of alternatives to self-mutilation in these situations.

The next step in making a relationship and the main body of this work, as described at the start of this chapter, is then establishing a relationship between the patient and therapist. It has been common in psychotherapy to see patients who self-mutilate as engaged in a struggle with the therapist whereby they demand that the therapist attend to and love them. In this work however, the therapist has to give the patient some form of an empathic bond, even though the patient may be after the 'wrong' kind of attachment (that is, desperate for the therapist to love her whilst at the same time not allowing the therapist to help her) as a result of her history, and may have been using the 'wrong' technique (self-mutilation) to achieve this.

Getting started in making a relationship may mean learning to communicate in a range of ways in addition to talking. The therapist may wish to introduce alternative media such as photography, or art where the resources are available. However, the therapist needs to be judicious in the use of these activities and needs to be aware of the danger of this representing a desperate casting about to find the means to 'get going'. The therapist, particularly one whose usual aim is to 'do something', needs to be very patient during this stage. The therapist may also have to identify and overcome her fear and her wish to distance herself from what may be horrifying material. She needs to be able to recognize the character of the horror of her patient's experience, if not its actual extent and to 'hear' and respond to the extent of the patient's distress.

Once the relational aspects are accomplished, and not before, the patient and therapist can move beyond their relationship into the perhaps more structured, definitely more difficult, area of making changes. The biggest, most important change is to seek to resolve and integrate the cause of the suffering that underlies self-mutilation.

Making changes

The cessation of the mutilating behaviour is not a target of therapy as we see it. However, once a relationship is established, the partners in the relationship can discuss making changes. Many of the changes made with people who self-injure are fundamentally the same as they would be in any other form of therapy, the only difference being that the patient needs to be in charge of whether or not self-mutilation is an issue.

Here again, the first and most fundamental change is to work towards making a patient who is unsafe, safe. Safety in the body is particularly important in this respect. People who self-injure feel unsafe in their bodies. Establishing safety begins by creating between patient and therapist a shared view of respect for the body. This may mean dealing with problems with sleep or eating. Patients and therapists engaged in this work may discuss exercise and basic health needs. Sometimes patients who self-injure are using prescribed medication. The therapist is not judgemental about the use of medication, but she is aware of the risk of reinforcing the idea that immediate physical solutions to pain and distress are desirable.

At this stage, combinations of therapeutic techniques can be used to manage stress, to alleviate extreme fears, or to deal with 'flashbacks' and other intrusions. Confusion, low mood states, and interpersonal difficulties can be addressed by structured cognitive strategies. Again, the therapist is judicious in her use of structured interventions, always aware of the importance of putting her patient fully in charge of her own recovery, and never introduces these interventions until a safe working relationship has been established. Cognitive work may focus on one or more of the following schema:

1. Self-mutilation is necessary to my survival;
   - it's my only option;
   - it's my only means of being taken seriously.
2. My body is disgusting/things to do with sex are disgusting.
3. I have to get rid of bad feelings immediately.

The purpose of these interventions is always to provide the patient with basic life skills, not to remove 'symptoms', and to prepare and enable the patient for the painful task of tackling the cause of the distress that lies beneath the symptoms. Trauma work in particular requires that the patient have in place sufficient internal and external resources to make it through the work safely.

At this point the therapy becomes more 'traditional' in the sense that underlying conflicts, painful memories and experiences may be discussed and their meaning comprehended. In the case of individuals who may self-mutilate severely this is likely to involve trauma work. It is not our intention here to summarize the totality of what this is likely to involve; instead, the reader is referred to Briere (1996); Courtois (1988); Herman (1992); Pearlman and Saakvitne (1995). We should like, however, to draw attention once more briefly to an aspect of psychotherapeutic work that has particular relevance in self-mutilation. The difficulty with verbal expressions of affect that underlies some instances of self-mutilation was discussed in *Chapter 4*. For such individuals, it becomes at once more compelling and at the same time more difficult to constitute a vocabulary through which to express distress. The talking that takes place in therapy can then lead to the same confusions and frustration as elsewhere in the patient's life. Babiker (1992) has suggested that the link between cognition and emotion as evidenced in processing of words relating to abuse, may be slowed down in individuals who have been abused. It could be, for some individuals, that a form of dissociation sets around certain words or certain topics. We feel that it is unlikely in such cases that an emphasis on expression about underlying trauma on either the therapist's or the patient's part, will be helpful. We concur with Judith Herman (1992) that the patient needs to 'stabilize' before any trauma material can be tackled. In the case of the patient with difficulties in verbalizing affect, and who utilizes somatic expressions of distress, we would suggest that the therapy attempts to create a frame in which to have 'ordinary' discussions about day-to-day relationships and what they mean to the patient, before moving on gradually to increasingly difficult material. This process itself is likely to take a long time, but has the advantage that it allows trust to develop and avoids persecuting the patient and recreating aspects of the abuse environment.

The ending of therapy

Ending therapy with a patient who self-injures is really no different from ending therapy with anyone else. There are difficult moments with endings for everyone. The therapist may worry about self-mutilation increasing during some of these difficult moments, but this is unlikely if the ending is timed appropriately, and processed adequately by both therapist and patient. What we have found, on those occasions when we have asked about self-mutilation towards the end of therapy, is that people report that they still sometimes think about it, but don't actually do it.

A major step of this final stage is to address the possible social alienation of the person who self-injures, in order to deliver them from therapy into the outside world. This is similar to establishing safety in the wider sense, and may include reviewing support systems, putting the patient in touch with voluntary agencies and self-help organizations, and encouraging the patient to initiate or expand her interests and activities in various areas.

Supervision for Those who Work with Self-Injury

The need for supervision in this area of work cannot be overstated. Much of the therapeutic work carried out with people who self-injure is concerned with the overlap between the area of maltreatment trauma, and the area of self-mutilation. In trauma work, the need for supervision has been explicitly and repeatedly stated. Pearlman and Saakvitne (1995), who have presented the most thorough and clear understanding of the needs of trauma therapists, underline throughout their book *Trauma and the Therapist* the necessity and essential nature of supervision in this work. It is our impression that individuals working in the trauma area understand the importance of supervision in their work, but may not always have the means, for internal or external reasons, to obtain the supervision they need. It is not the intention of this chapter to cover comprehensively the issues involved in supervising trauma work. Rather, what we hope to deal with is the theme of how the need for supervision applies particularly to working with self-mutilation. It will become clear that here again within the area of one-to-one therapy supervision, we are interested in delineating different *levels* of supervisory work ranging from direct teaching through to dealing with the clinician's own exposure to trauma via the patient's self-mutilation.

Model of supervision

There is a trend now in clinical work away from one up-one down models of supervision where a more experienced therapist addresses another's inexperience, towards more egalitarian models of the process where therapist and supervisor are seen as working together towards understanding the therapeutic process and addressing the therapist's difficulties. This model is sometimes particularly appropriate in 'new' fields of clinical work such as maltreatment trauma work and self-mutilation, where more and less experienced therapists are discovering and formulating clinical problems together. Equally, the traditional model may work better in some cases. There is more anxiety in a more 'equal' model for both therapist and supervisor. In cases where a therapist is encountering severe self-injury for the first time and feels overwhelmed, it may be reassuring to rely on more directive guidance from a more experienced clinician in this area of work.

Issues for the therapist

Pearlman and Saakvitne (1995) see trauma therapy supervision as supervision not of a 'case' but of a *relationship*, between the therapist and the patient. When seen this way, the focus changes. We suggested that the therapist should monitor and note her reactions to the details of her patients' self-injury, to take to supervision. The supervisory relationship raises further issues that the partners in the supervision may also wish to monitor:

1. the therapist may not have encountered self-injury before;
2. the therapist may have to contain more of her own anxiety than she is used to;
3. the therapist may never have *not* intervened with a distressing 'symptom' or problem behaviour before;
4. the therapist may feel the cutting to be an attempt to manipulate her;
5. the therapist may perceive the behaviour as intended to punish her;
6. the self-injury may increase during therapy.

Issues for the supervisor

In working with self-mutilation, the supervisor needs to hold the theoretical and philosophical approaches and employ these to contain the therapist's anxiety. Yet the supervisor may not always want to be seen as an expert who has all the answers when she herself is feeling overwhelmed.

The supervisor who directs a therapist to 'hold' her patient's self-injury instead of seeking to stop it may find that this is extremely difficult for the therapist to undertake. These difficulties may then be translated into anger at the supervisor. Our experience, and that of others (for example, Zerbe, 1988) suggests that this situation works best when the supervisor is respectful and validating of the therapist, but ultimately has the responsibility for determining the approach towards the patient's self-mutilation.

The supervisor can experience accounts of self-injury reported by the therapist as traumatizing. To hear these descriptions out of the context of knowing the patient and having regular contact with them may leave the supervisor vulnerable. In the course of our work together each of the authors of this book has had this experience, where accounts of forms of mutilation reported by the other were more disturbing than those of people we had each worked with.

The process

The process of supervision in this area raises the following points:

1. Episodes of self-injury do not form the focus of the supervision, any more than they do the therapy. However, as the reactions of others involved in a case impact on the therapist, the supervisor is a very important source of support and validation when the therapist has to defend her approach.

2. When the system demands that the symptom be brought under control this can evoke feelings in the therapist that closely mirror those of her patient, and supervision can help identify these and clarify their usefulness in the therapy.

3. Over-investment: the therapist needs to be protected from the need to endlessly re-parent, to protect her patient from her own impulses, become exhausted and endanger the treatment of others.

4. The therapist needs to be protected from the sense of being tyrannized by the patient's self-mutilation.

5. Under-investment: being cared for enables the therapist to convey a sense of care that the patient previously lacked. This is what allows the therapist to present a 'holding environment' and overcomes the therapist's need to distance herself.

6. The supervisor can 'absorb' concerns relating to confidentiality and risk assessment.

7. The therapist may see implied criticism in the supervision process: as the prescription is to not be horrified by or try to prevent this behaviour, if the therapist experiences either of these, she may feel inadequate. It can also be difficult for the therapist to deal with the feelings engendered by a supervisor who has 'all the knowledge', particularly of such an upsetting behaviour as self-mutilation, and the feelings of shame and outrage can lead to resistance of further supervision; or to disagreement.

8. Personal therapy: if supervision is taken up excessively with issues that relate to the therapist's own history, then personal therapy is indicated. If the therapist herself has been a victim of serious trauma which remains unresolved, or if the therapist also self-mutilates, then personal therapy is essential.

Conclusion: Towards Transformation

We have said that self-injury is a language which we as helpers are called upon to comprehend in all its meanings. It speaks of an individual's pain and struggle. It also tells of the social, cultural and political circumstances in which they and we find ourselves. Failings and injustices in the services may also be expressed to us through an individual's self-injuring, and our response to this is complicated by the fact that we are part of these very services. We are called upon to extend our understanding of self-injury to the paradox of how a person can use their body to preserve and express themselves, even as they are hurting and violating the body.

In doing this work, we are required to bear witness to great individual pain, despair, anger, loss and longing, and to attempt to make meaning of these experiences. We need also to find the courage to acknowledge difficult truths about oppression, injustice and cruelty in the world in which we live. This will remind us of our own struggles, and our own experiences of distress and powerlessness, with which we too need help and support. In the therapeutic relationship, the patient is not the only one who feels pain, nor the only one for whom transformation is possible.

In the relationship between helper and sufferer, there are rewards for both. Both are taking part in a process by which the unspeakable becomes spoken, because it is now both bearable and possible to speak it. In speaking of one's experience to another, who comprehends that experience and allows it to touch them, there lies the possibility of no longer being imprisoned by that experience, in one's body or one's life.

References

Aldridge, D. (1988). Treating Self-Mutilating Behavior: A social strategy. *Family Systems Medicine, 6(1),* 5–20.

Alexander, F. (1929). The need for punishment and the death instinct. *International Journal of Psychoanalysis, 10,* 260. (Cited in K.A. Menninger (1938) *Man Against Himself.* London: Rupert Hart-Davis (Harvest Books).)

Arnold, L. and Magill, A. (1996). *Working with Self-Injury: A Practical Guide.* Bristol: The Basement Project.

Arnold, L. and Magill, A. (1996). *Strength in Numbers: Groupwork with women abused in childhood.* Bristol: The Basement Project.

Arnold, L. (1995). *Women and Self-Injury: A survey of 76 women.* Bristol: Bristol Crisis Service for Women.

Babiker, G. (1992). *Psychological Measurement and the Identification of Sexual Abuse in Children and Adolescents.* Unpublished Ph.D. thesis, University of Bristol.

Babiker, G. (1995). *Therapy with Women Who Self-Injure.* Workshop at Conference: 'Cutting Out the Pain'. Bristol, September 1995.

Babiker, G. and Herbert, M. (1996). The role of psychological instruments in the assessment of child sexual abuse. *Child Abuse Review, 5,* 239–251.

Babiker, I.E. (1993). Managing sexual abuse disclosure by adult psychiatric patients – some suggestions. *Psychiatric Bulletin, 17,* 286–288.

Bach-Y-Rita, G. (1974). Habitual violence and self-mutilation. *American Journal of Psychiatry, 131,* 1018–1020.

Beliappa, J. (1991). *Illness or Distress? Alternative Models of Mental Health.* London: Confederation of Indian Organisations.

Bollas, C.B. (1995). *Cracking Up: The work of unconscious experience.* London: Routledge.

Bradford, D.T. (1990). Early Christian martyrdom and the psychology of depression, suicide, and bodily mutilation. Special Issue: Psychotherapy and religion. *Psychotherapy and Psychosomatics, 27(1),* 30–41.

Briere, J., Henschel, D., Smiljanich, K. and Morgan-Magallanes, M. (1990). Conference abstract: Self-injurious behaviour and child abuse history in adult men and women. Paper presented at the National Symposium on Child Victimization, Atlanta.

Briere, J. (1996). *Therapy for Adults Molested as Children: Beyond survival (2nd edn).* New York: Springer Publishing.

Bunclark, J. (1996). *Allowing Choices.* Paper presented at Conference 'Working With Self-injury', Durham, May 1996.

Burrow, S. (1992). The deliberate self-harming behaviour of patients within a British special hospital. *Journal of Advanced Nursing, 17,* 138–148.

Burstow, B. (1992). *Radical Feminist Therapy.* Newbury Park: Sage.

Carr, E.G. and Durand, V.M. (1985). The social communicative basis of severe behavior problems in children. In S. Reiss and R.R. Bootzin (Eds) *Theoretical Issues in Behavior Therapy.* New York: Academic Press.

Chasseguet-Smirgel, J. (1990). On acting out. *International Journal of Psychoanalysis, 71,* 77–86.

Connerton, P. (1989). *How Societies Remember.* Cambridge: Cambridge University Press.

Cook, D. and Babiker, G. (1995). *Guidelines for Professionals in UBHT Working with Adult Psychiatric Patients who Disclose Sexual Abuse in Childhood.* United Bristol Healthcare Trust, Mental Health Directorate.

Cookson, H.M. (1977). A survey of self-injury in a closed prison for women. *British Journal of Criminology. 17(4),* 332–334.

Courtois, C. (1988). *Healing the Incest Wound: Adult survivors in therapy.* New York: Norton and Co.

Cross, L.W. (1993). Body and self in feminine development: implications for eating disorders and delicate self-mutilation. *Bulletin of the Menninger Clinic, 57(1),* 41–68

Csordas, T.J. (1994). *Embodiment and experience: The existential ground of culture and self.* Cambridge: Cambridge University Press.

Cullen, J.E. (1985). Prediction and treatment of self-injury by female young offenders. In D.P. Tarrington and R.Tarling (Eds) *Prediction in Criminology.* Albany: State University of New York Press.

Davies, D. and Neal, C. (1996). *Pink Therapy.* Buckingham: Open University Press.

de Young, M. (1982). *The Sexual Victimization of Children.* London: McFarland and Co.

Dieter, P.J. and Pearlman, L.A. (in press). Responding to Self-Injurious Behaviour. In P. Kleespies (Ed.) *Emergencies in Mental Health Practice: Evaluation and management.* New York: Guilford Publications.

Favazza, A.R. (1987). *Bodies Under Siege.* Baltimore: Johns Hopkins University Press.

Favazza, A.R. (1989). Why patients mutilate themselves. *Hospital and Community Psychiatry, 40 (2),* 137–145.

Favazza, A.R. (1992). Repetitive self-mutilation. *Psychiatric Annals, 22(2),* 60–63.

Favazza, A.R. and Rosenthal, R.J. (1993). Diagnostic issues in self-mutilation. *Hospital and Community Psychiatry, 44(2),* 134–140.

Favazza, A.R., De Rosear, L., and Conterio, K. (1989). Self-mutilation and eating disorders. *Suicide and Life-Threatening Behavior, 19(4),* 352–361.

Feldman, M.D. and Ford, C.V. (1994). *Patient or Pretender: Inside the strange world of factitious disorder.* New York: Wiley.

Feldman, M.D. (1988). The challenge of self-mutilation: a review. *Comprehensive Psychiatry, 29(3),* 252–269.

Fonagy, P. (1991). Thinking about thinking: some clinical and theoretical considerations in the treatment of a borderline patient. *International Journal of Psychoanalysis, 72,* 639–656.

Fonagy, P. and Target, M. (1995). Understanding the violent patient: The use of the body and the role of the father. *International Journal of Psychoanalysis, 76,* 487–501.

Fossum, M.A. and Mason, M.J. (1986). *Facing Shame: Families in recovery.* New York: WW Norton and Co.

Frances, A. (1987). The borderline self-mutilator: introduction. *Journal of Personality Disorders, 1,* 316.

Gardner, D.L. and Cowdrey, R.W. (1985). Suicidal and parasuicidal behaviour in borderline personality disorder. *Psychiatric Clinics of North America, 8,* 389–403.

Geist, R.A. (1979). Onset of chronic illness in children and adolescents. *American Journal of Orthopsychiatry, 52,* 704–711.

German, G.A. (1987). A neurobiological hypothesis on the nature of chronic self-mutilation. *Integrated Psychiatry, 4,* 212–213.

Gil, E. (1988). *Treatment of Adult Survivors of Childhood Abuse.* Walnut Creek, CA: Launch Press.

Girard, R. (1977). *Violence and the Sacred.* Baltimore: Johns Hopkins University Press.

Graff, H. and Mallin, R. (1967). The syndrome of the wrist-cutter. *American Journal of Psychiatry, 135,* 579–582.

Green, A.H. (1987). Self-destructive behavior in battered children. *American Journal of Psychiatry, 135,* 579–582.

Greenspan, G.S. and Samuel, S.E. (1989). Self-cutting after rape. *American Journal of Psychiatry, 146,* 789–790.

Gunderson, J.G. and Singer, M.T. (1986). Defining borderline patients: an overview. In M.H. Stone (Ed.) *Essential Papers on Borderline Disorders: One hundred years at the border.* New York: New York University Press.

Haines, J., Williams, C.L., Brain, K.L. and Wilson, G.V. (1995). The psychobiology of self-mutilation. *Journal of Abnormal Psychology, 104(3),* 471–489.

Harry, B. (1987). Tattoos, body experience, and body image boundary among violent male offenders. *Bulletin of the American Academy of Psychiatry and the Law, 15(2),* 171–178.

Harrison, D. (1996). *Vicious Circles.* London: Good Practices in Mental Health.

Herman, J. (1992). *Trauma and Recovery: From domestic abuse to political terror.* London: Pandora.

HMSO (1990). Home Office Research Study No 115, *Suicide and Self-injury in Prison: A literature review.* London: HMSO.

Holloway Project Committee (1985). *Holloway Project Committee Report.* H.M. Prison Service. London: HMSO.

Holmes, J. (1995). Supportive psychotherapy: the search for positive meanings. *British Journal of Psychiatry, 167,* 439–445.

Hughes, M.C. (1982). Chronically ill children in groups: recurrent issues and adaptations. *American Journal of Orthopsychiatry, 52*, 704–711.

Kelland, D. (1995). *Working with Women who Self-injure: Therapeutic Optimism v. Therapeutic Pessimism.* A study of self-injury amongst women in Holloway prison, submitted for M.Sc. in Applied Criminological Psychology, Birkbeck College. Unpublished paper.

Kernberg, O. (1967). Borderline personality organization. *Journal of the American Psychoanalytic Association, 15*, 641–685.

Kreitman, N. (1977). *Parasuicide.* Chichester: Wiley.

Lacey, J.H. (1993). Self-damaging and addictive behaviour in bulimia nervosa: a catchment area study. *British Journal of Psychiatry, 163*, 190–194.

Lacey, J.H. and Evans, C.D.H. (1986). The impulsivist: a multi-impulsive personality disorder. *British Journal of Addiction, 81*, 641–649.

Liebling, H. and Chipchase, H. (1993). *A Pilot Study on the Problem of Self-injurious Behaviour in Women in Ashworth Hospital.* (Unpublished manuscript.)

Liebling, H., Chipchase, H. and Velangi, R. (1996). *Women who Self-Harm in in a Special Hospital.* (Unpublished manuscript.)

Lindberg, F.H. and Distad, J. (1985). Survival responses to incest: adolescents in crisis. *Child Abuse and Neglect, 9*, 521–526.

Lindsay, H. (1995). Needing Attention: an evaluation of services for women who self-injure. Bristol: Bristol Crisis Service for Women.

Linehan, M.M. (1993). *Cognitive-Behavioural Treatment of Borderline Personality Disorder.* New York: Guilford Press.

Littlewood, R. and Cross, S. (1980). Ethnic minorities and psychiatric services. *Sociology of Health and Illness, 2(2)*, 194–201.

Lyons, J.A. (1991). Self-mutilation by a man with post-traumatic stress disorder. *Journal of Nervous and Mental Disease, 179(8)*, 505–507.

McCann, I.L. and Pearlman, L.A. (1990). *Psychological Trauma and the Adult Survivor: Theory, therapy, and transformation.* New York: Bruner Mazel.

McGovern, D. and Cope, R. (1987). Compulsory detention of males of different ethnic groups with special reference to offender status. *British Journal of Psychiatry, 150*, 505–512.

Menninger, K. (1938). *Man Against Himself.* London: Rupert Hart-Davis (Harvest Books).

Merril, J. and Owens, J. (1986). Ethnic differences in self-poisoning: a comparison of Asian and White groups. *British Journal of Psychiatry, 148*, 708–712.

Miller, D. (1994). *Women Who Hurt Themselves: A book of hope and understanding.* New York: Basic Books.

Mollon, P. (1996). *Multiple Selves, Multiple Voices: Working with trauma violation and dissociation.* London: John Wiley and Sons.

Morgan, H.G. (1979). *Death Wishes? The understanding and management of deliberate self-harm.* London: Wiley.

Muluka, E. (1986). Severe self-mutilation among Kenyan psychotics. *British Journal of Psychiatry, 149*, 778–780.

Nelson, S. and Grunebaum, H. (1971). A follow-up study of wrist-slashers. *American Journal of Psychiatry, 127*, 1345–1349.

Nemiah, J.C. and Sifneos, P.E. (1970). Psychosomatic illness: a problem of communication. *Psychotherapy and Psychosomatics, 18*, 154–160.

Offer, D. and Barglow, P. (1960). Adolescent and young adult self-mutilation incidents in a general psychiatric hospital. *Archives of General Psychiatry, 3*, 194–204.

Pao, P.E. (1969). The syndrome of delicate self-cutting. *British Journal of Medical Psychology, 42*, 195–206.

Parkin, J.R. and Eagles, J.M. (1993). Blood-letting in bulimia nervosa. *British Journal of Psychiatry, 162*, 246–248.

Pattison, E.M. and Kahan, J. (1983). The deliberate self-harm syndrome. *American Journal of Psychiatry, 140*, 867–872.

Pawlicki, C.M. and Gaumer, C. (1993). Nursing care of the self-mutilating patient. *Bulletin of the Menninger Clinic, 57(3)*, 380–389.

Pearlman, L.A. and Saakvitne, K.W. (1995). *Trauma and the Therapist: Countertransference and vicarious traumatization in psychotherapy with incest survivors.* New York: W.W. Norton and Co.

Pembroke, L. (Ed.) (1994). *Self-Harm: Perspectives from Personal Experience.* London: Survivors Speak Out.

Pembroke, L. (1996). *Self-injury: Myths and common sense.* London: National Self-Harm Network.

Pembroke , L. and Smith, A. (1996). *Minimising the Damage from Self-harm.* London: National Self-Harm Network .

Pines, D. (1993). *A Woman's Unconscious Use of her Body: A psychoanalytical perspective.* London: Virago.

Pines, D. (1980). Skin communication: early skin disorders and their effect on transference and countertransference. *International Journal of Psychoanalysis, 61*, 315–322.

Pitman, R.K. (1990). Self-mutilation in combat-related PTSD. *American Journal of Psychiatry, 147*, 123–124.

Potier, M.A. (1993). Giving evidence: women's lives in Ashworth Maximum Security Psychiatric Hospital. *Feminism and Psychology, 3(3)*, 335–347.

Robinson, C. (1996). Personal communication.

Rockland, L.H. (1987). A supportive approach: psychodynamically oriented supportive therapy-treatment of borderline patients who self-mutilate. *Journal of Personality Disorders, 1(4)*, 350–353.

Ross, R.R. and McKay, H.B. (1979). *Self-mutilation.* Lexington, MA: Lexington Books.

Senior, N. (1988). Families of suicidal and non-suicidal self-mutilating adolescents. *Family Therapy, 15(1)* 31–37.

Sgroi, S.M. (1982). *Handbook of Clinical Intervention in Child Sexual Abuse.* Lexington, MA: Lexington Books.

Shapiro, S. (1987). Self-mutilation and self-blame in incest victims. *American Journal of Psychotherapy, XLI (1)*, 46–54.

Sifneos, P.E. (1972). The prevalence of 'alexythemic' characteristics in psychosomatic patients. In H. Freyberger (Ed.) *Topics of Psychosomatic Research.* Basle: Karger.

Simeon, D., Stanley, B., Frances, A., Mann, J.J., Winchel, R., and Stanley, M. (1992). Self-mutilation in personality disorders: psychological and biological correlates. *American Journal of Psychiatry, 149*, 221–226.

Simpson, A. and Ng, M. (1992). Deliberate self-harm of Filipino immigrants in Hong Kong. *Psychologia: An International Journal of Psychology in the Orient, 35*, 117–120.

Simpson, M.A. (1976). Self-mutilation. *British Journal of Hospital Medicine, 16*, 430–438.

Simpson, M.A. (1977). Self-mutilation and borderline syndrome. *Dynamische Psychiatrie, 42*, 42–48. (Cited in S. Shapiro, (1987).

Soni Raleigh V. and Balarajan, R. (1992). Suicide and self-burning among Indians and West Indians in England and Wales. *British Journal of Psychiatry, 161*, 365–368.

Spandler, H. (1996). *Who's Hurting Who? Young people, self-harm and suicide.* Manchester: 42nd Street.

Stimpson, L. and Best, M. (1991). *Courage Above All: Sexual assault against women with disability.* Toronto: DisAbled Women's Network (DAWN).

Stone, M.H. (1987). A psychodynamic approach: some thoughts on the dynamics and therapy of self-mutilating borderline patients. *Journal of Personality Disorders, 1(4)*, 347–349.

Tantam, D. and Whittaker, J. (1992). Personality disorder and self-wounding. *British Journal of Psychiatry, 161*, 451–464.

Toch, H. (1975). *Men in Crisis.* Chicago: Aldine.

Trenchard, L. and Warren, H. (1984). *Something to Tell You.* London: London Gay Teenage Group.

van der Kolk, B.A. (1988). The trauma spectrum: the interaction of biological and social events in the genesis of the trauma response. *Journal of Traumatic Stress, 1*, 273–290.

van der Kolk, B.A., Perry, C. and Herman, J. (1991). Childhood origins of self-destructive behaviour. *American Journal of Psychiatry, 148(12)*, 1665–1671.

van der Kolk, B.A., McFarlane, A.C. and Weisaeth, L. (1996). *Traumatic Stress: The effects of an overwhelming experience on mind, body and society.* New York: Guilford Press.

van der Kolk B.A. and Fisler, R. (1995). Dissociation and the fragmentary nature of traumatic memories: overview and exploratory study. *Journal of Traumatic Stress, 8*, 505–525.

Walsh, B.W. and Rosen, P.M. (1988). *Self-Mutilation: Theory, Research and Treatment.* New York: Guilford Press.

Weissman, M. (1975). Wrist cutting. *Archives of General Psychiatry, 32*, 1166–1171.

Weldon, E. (1996). Perversions in men and women. *British Journal of Psychotherapy, 12(4)*, 480–486.

Westcott, H. (1991). The abuse of disabled children: a review of the literature. *Child: Care, health and development, 17*, 243–258.

Winchel, R.M. and Stanley, M. (1991) Self-injurious behavior: A review of the behavior and biology of self-mutilation. *American Journal of Psychiatry, 148(3)*, 306–317.

Wise, W.L. (1989). Adult self-injury as a survival response in victim-survivors of childhood abuse. *Journal of Chemical Dependency Treatment, 3(1)*, 185-201.

Women's Support Project (1995). *'We're no exception': Male violence against women with disability.* A report for the Zero Tolerance Campaign. Glasgow: Women's Support Project.

Young, L. (1992). Sexual abuse and the problem of embodiment. *Child Abuse and Neglect, 16*, 89–100.

Zerbe, K.J. (1988). Walking on the razor's edge: the use of consultation in the treatment of a self-mutilating patient. *Bulletin of the Menninger Clinic, 52*, 492–503.

Appendix 1: Resources

The Basement Project: 82 Colston St., Bristol BS1 5BB. Telephone 0117 922 5801. Groupwork/workshops, training, research and literature concerning self-injury and abuse. Helpful publications include: *Working with self-injury: a practical guide; What's the harm? A book for young people who self-harm or self-injure.*

Bristol Crisis Service for Women: PO Box 654, Bristol BS99 1XH. Telephone 0117 925 1119. Helpline, research and publications on self-injury. Training pack available. Hold details of other projects and groups around the UK with a focus on self-injury. Helpful booklets available include: *Understanding self-injury; Self-help for self-injury; For friends and family.*

MIND (National Association for Mental Health): Granta House, 15–19 Broadway, London E15 4BQ. Telephone 0181 519 2122. Information, details of local services. Helpful pamphlet available: *Understanding self-harm.*

National Self-harm Network: c/o S.S.O. 34 Osnaburgh St., London NW1 3ND. Campaigning group for people who self-harm/self-injure. Developing guidelines for good practice in services for people who self-injure. Meetings, information and literature.

SHOUT: c/o Box 654, Bristol BS99 1XH. Bimonthly newsletter for women who self-harm, and supporters.

Index

Compiled by Mary Kirkness